21st Century Legal C‍
By Richard L. Hermann

Overview: Where the Jobs Are
The Hottest Attorney and JD-Advantage Opportunities

Volume 1
Data Protection Practice: The Brave New Legal World

Volume 2
Careers in Compliance: JDs Wanted

Volume 3
Health Law: Career Opportunities in a Fast-Changing
Environment

Volume 4
Energy Law: Fueling a Dynamic Legal Career

Volume 5
"Soft" Intellectual Property Law: IP Opportunities for
Non-STEM Attorneys

Volume 6
Risk Management: The Indispensable Profession

Volume 7
The Administrative Law Revolution: Learning to Litigate
in a Forgiving Environment

For additional booklet topics, updates and, legal career news visit http://legalcareerview.com

21st Century Legal Career Series
Volume 12

JD Advantage Jobs in Corporations
Expanding the Legal Function

Richard L. Hermann

Published by H Watson Consulting LLC

To inquire about booking Richard L. Hermann to speak on 21st Century Legal Career Series content or other legal career management topics, contact donna@legalcareerview.com.

Cover design by Aaron Payne, aaron@awdience.com
Book design by Chris Rubio, info@thegeekfather.rocks

ISBN #978-1-946228-23-9

To today's law students, who have many more career opportunities from which to choose than at any time in history.

Contents

About the Author

Richard L. Hermann graduated from Yale, the New School University, and Cornell Law School (following a stint in the U.S. Army, where he handled nuclear weapons and jumped out of airplanes). His first job out of law school was as an attorney at the Pentagon. He went on to work for the Government Accountability Office and Department of Energy. During his brief government career, he counseled friends and acquaintances on finding government law jobs, which evolved into launching Federal Reports Inc. The company became the leading provider of legal career information in the U.S. Among its many products were AttorneyJobs.com, LawStudentJobsOnline.com, and many other legal career publications and web products (all now the property of Thomson Reuters).

He also founded and led Nationwide Career Counseling for Attorneys and Sutherland Hermann Associates, an attorney outplacement and disability insurance consulting firm. Later he developed and taught the first law school course in *Legal Career Management* for online Concord Law School. He is also a regular columnist for *National Jurist*.

In the 1990s, he wrote three editions of *JD Preferred: 600+ Jobs You Can Do with a Law Degree (Other Than Practice Law)*. Today that number is 1,000+.

Legal Career View (http://legalcareerview.com) is Hermann's latest addition to his body of work on legal careers (both traditional and non-mainstream [a.k.a. "JD-Advantage]). *Legal*

Career View helps you connect the dots between today's news and tomorrow's jobs, shares Hermann's treasure trove of legal employment blogs, answers your questions, and provides strategies for securing a rewarding career in—and around—the law.

In addition to this **21st Century Legal Career Series**, Richard Hermann publications include:

- *Manufacturing Business and the Law: A Guide to the Laws, Regulations, and Careers of the U.S. Manufacturing Revival* (American Bar Association [ABA], 2015). 758 pp. $129.95; ABA Member Price: $103.95
- *Practicing Law in Small-Town America* (ABA, 2012). 498 pp. $99.95; ABA Member Price: $79.95
- *Landing a Federal Legal Job: Finding Success in the U.S. Government Job Market* (ABA, 2011). 552 pp. $69.95; ABA Member Price: $54.95
- *Managing Your Legal Career: Best Practices for Creating the Career You Want* (finalist for Best Career Book, 2010) (ABA, 2010). 424 pp. $69.95; ABA Member Price: $54.95 All at http://shop.americanbar.org/ebus/store.aspx?term=Hermann
- *From Lemons to Lemonade in the New Legal Job Market: Winning Job-Search Strategies for Entry-Level Attorneys* (Decision Books, 2012). 254 pp. $30.00 from the National Association for Law Placement (http://nalp.org/bookstore).
- *The Lawyer's Guide to Job Security* (Kaplan Publishing, 2010). 240 pp. $28.31 from Amazon.com (http://amazon.com).

- *The Lawyer's Guide to Finding Success in Any Job Market* (Kaplan Publishing, 2009). 288 pp. $3.49 from Amazon.com (www.amazon.com) and BarnesandNoble.com (http://barnesandnoble.com)

Hermann's , *Encounters: Appointments with History,* published by Persimmon Alley Press, is also scheduled for release in 2017.

Focus: What This Booklet Is All About

This booklet examines the impressive range and growing diversity of JD Advantage jobs in corporations open to individuals who have a law degree.

By the time a law student graduates from law school, s/he probably understands that the vast majority of corporations do not hire entry-level attorneys for traditional law practice positions in their in-house counsel offices. This is particularly true of publicly-traded and large privately-held companies, of which there are approximately 6,000 of the former and more than 2,000 of the latter, which together comprise a small percentage of the more than 6 million U.S. corporations. Smaller companies are also loath to hire newly-minted lawyers lacking in experience for their general counsel offices.

What very few law students realize is that this should not deter them from including corporations in their job-search strategy portfolio. Since the late 1970s, American companies have embarked on a major expansion of their legal hiring to include thousands of attorneys who work in JD Advantage positions in corporate offices and roles other than just their traditional, mainstream legal office(s). This development has accelerated in the 21st century. Today you will find attorneys in multiple corporate offices that, in many cases, did not exist a generation ago.

These offices often have a much lower "experience bar" when it comes to recruitment and hiring, which opens up many jobs to qualified recent law graduates. Moreover, once you have your foot in the corporate door, opportunities to advance within the company and across legal and quasi-legal functions improve significantly.

In addition to JD Advantage jobs in the many corporate offices you will encounter in this booklet, the number of positions preferring individuals with a law degree in non-legal or quasi-legal corporate divisions is also expanding. This is particularly true with respect to attorneys who bring something in addition to their law degree to the table, such as an undergraduate degree or work experience in fields such as business, marketing, finance, economics, accounting, human capital, e-business, knowledge management, consulting, project management, operations management, organizational behavior, risk analysis, STEM, etc. These lawyers can be found today across industries, corporate cultures, and business lines. The number of corporate positions preferring such a "combination" background advertised online has jumped by more than 200 percent in the last five years.

This booklet is intended to show candidates where to look for JD Advantage jobs in corporations. The information is based on the author's 30-plus years advising thousands of JDs who successfully transitioned from law school and mainstream law to corporate JD Advantage positions. The booklet is *data-driven*, based on the specific experiences and track record of actual attorneys who successfully sought such positions and thrive in them.

Why Are Corporate JD Advantage Jobs So Hot?

My career advising and assisting thousands of attorneys and law students negotiate the legal employment market prompted me to develop a *Practice Area Analysis Template* designed to enable legal job seekers to determine if a particular practice area is a good bet or something to avoid. My goal was to incorporate actual data into the usual speculation rampant in legal trade journals and proffered continuously by self-styled "experts," often on no other basis than a gut feeling or a smattering of anecdotal evidence. The *Template*, in contrast, permits us to identify a practice area as "hot" because it allows for an educated conclusion based on an unbiased factual examination of the data.

This section applies the *Template* criteria to corporate JD Advantage jobs.

Note. It is not necessary that all 10 metrics below be met for a practice area to pass the "hotness" test. However, the more metrics that are met, the hotter the practice area is likely to be. It is worth a legal job seeker's attention if a majority of the criteria are satisfied.

1. **Supply and Demand.** *Ideally, the demand for individuals who can do the work should exceed the supply of qualified individuals.*

   The demand for JD Advantage lawyers in U.S. corporations is escalating because of the following factors:

- *Complexity.* The world is not becoming simpler or easier to understand and negotiate. Quite the contrary. The 21st century has focused increasing attention on a variety of new issues and risks that have complicated life for both individuals and organizations. A constant flood of federal and state legislation and regulations, major court decisions that have altered business models, and the massive restructuring of entire industries in order to remain competitive, add to the byzantine mix.
- *Globalization.* Interconnectedness across borders is the new normal. Corporations are increasingly multinational. Supply chains and manufacturing processes meander all over the world before there is a finished product. The simple T-shirt is a classic example of this and worth examination because it demonstrates as well as anything how globalization affects companies. While producing a T-shirt may appear to be a simple process, it is actually quite complex, involving nine discrete steps which, in the extreme, could involve nine (or more) different countries:
  - *Farming.* Most T-shirts are cotton, so cotton farming is step one. Cotton grows in narrow climactic bands around the world, thus there are only a few places where a manufacturer can obtain the raw material for its T-shirts.
  - *Ginning* involves separating the cotton (lint) from the seed and compressing it into bales for shipment.

- *Spinning* requires a number of machines that turn the cotton into yarn.
- *Knitting* turns the yarn into cloth by pulling loops of cotton rope through one another, with a separate cloth tube needed for each garment size.
- *Finishing* is a multi-step process that begins with washing out any particulate matter, bleaching or dyeing the knit cloth to a consistent color, shrinking the fabric, and softening it to prevent holes from opening up when sewed.
- *Cutting.* Bodies, sleeves, and collars are cut out of the fabric tube.
- *Sewing* is very labor-intensive (thus its disproportionate presence in low-wage countries), requiring one individual to operate each sewing machine.
- *Printing.* T-shirt panels are printed using screen-printing, spray painting, digital printing, or heat embossing.
- *Dyeing.* This final step adds more value to the product, and only takes place if the T-shirt has not been dyed during finishing. Once dyed, the T-shirt is shipped to the retailer.

- *Technology.* Innovation and its frequent consequence, "creative destruction," are increasing and often result in business models that become obsolete overnight (see, e.g., fax machines and video rental stores). Businesses have to be super-agile in order to survive the 21st century technological onslaught.

- *Demographics.* Baby boomers and millennials between them constitute a 160-million person market with money to spend. Companies have to respond to these mega-markets that change on a dime as they make their way through life.
- *Turmoil.* Uncertainty and unpredictability have replaced the sure, straight path that used to be the corporate comfort zone. In just the 21st century alone, fully one-third of the companies that comprise the Dow Jones Industrials are new.
- *Track Record.* Company executives have come to realize that the attorneys they hire for these law-related jobs are smart, analytical, articulate, and very hard workers. That makes them attractive employees for positions other than mainstream law.

Overall, this means more JD Advantage jobs are available than ever before.

2. **Number of Job Opportunities.** *The discipline should offer a large number of job opportunities relative to other practice options.*

The U.S. is home to 6,000 public companies and 6 million closely-held corporations, plus tens of thousands of nonprofit corporations that also offer a multitude of diverse JD Advantage job opportunities. Consequently, the number of JD Advantage job opportunities open at any given time is immense.

3. **Sustainability.** *The discipline should not be a flash in the pan. It should exhibit signs that it will be around beyond the present.*

Corporate JD Advantage jobs are not only increasing in number, but also in popularity. The example of their success in large companies is trickling down into smaller companies and across additional functional lines in larger ones, prompting corporate managers to look for other areas where attorneys might contribute and thrive. All of the factors cited above (see Metric #1) are going to continue to generate new opportunities in both existing and new areas of corporate endeavor.

4. **An Upward Curve.** *The practice should be a growth industry with a positive long-term outlook.*

   Both the number of corporations and the complexity of their organizational charts are growing along with the laws, regulations and external threats that make their businesses more complex and even jeopardize their survival. This means more JD Advantage opportunities down the line.

5. **Geographic Scope.** *Jobs should be available nationwide, or at least in a large number of geographic locations.*

   Corporate JD Advantage jobs are everywhere, primarily concentrated in larger communities. However, it is also possible to find them in less populous areas and in employment sectors that are often located in small towns and rural areas, such as community colleges, community banks, and hospitals.

6. **Relative Ease of Entry**. *The learning curve should not be too steep to be conquered by a novice. Some affordable education or training should be available to supplement basic legal education and experience.*

   Corporations hire a significant number of attorneys for certain JD Advantage positions directly out of law school. Contract and procurement jobs, for example, are replete with novice lawyers. Young lawyers can also gain a competitive edge by supplementing their law degrees with inexpensive and non-time-consuming certificate and comparable programs. (See *Positioning Yourself for a Corporate JD Advantage Job.*)

7. **Ideally, It Should Be New or Different**. *The discipline should allow for opportunities for practitioners to be among those who are "first-past-the-post."*

   While corporate law is of ancient origin, some of the new areas of corporate concern that have resulted in the creation of JD Advantage jobs are of recent vintage. Privacy and Data Protection positions, for example, are just getting their feet wet.

8. **Distinctive Value Proposition/Competitive Advantage**. *Knowledge should be able to provide the elements of a unique selling proposition for future job campaigns.*

   JD Advantage jobs in companies vary with respect to their marketability. Those that deal with the most pressing and vexing issues are, of course, the most marketable. Data protection is a prime example. There is both a huge market and desperate need for individuals who understand this sometimes existential threat (see, e.g., Volume 1 in the *21st Century Legal Career* Series entitled *Data Protection Practice: The Brave New Legal World*). That gives this discipline a lot of moxie and impetus.

9. **Threat Analysis.** *Is this discipline potentially subject to substitution of a human lawyer by a disruptive technology, legal process outsourcing...or something else? And how soon could this happen?*

   Those corporate functions in which JD Advantage attorneys work that are more ministerial and less dependent on human judgment might, down the line, be at risk of being wholly or partially replaced by software or artificial intelligence. For example, fields reliant on numbers and their manipulation lend themselves more readily to potential substitution of human beings by machines.

10. **Compensation.** *Will this field allow someone to manage their student debt effectively?*

    Compensation for these jobs varies dramatically based on the following factors: type of job; geographic location; size of company; intensity of demand; and more. (See *What Do Corporate JD Advantage Jobs Pay?*)

Selected JD Advantage Job Titles and Work Environments

Companies, primarily large, publicly-traded ones, are where most corporate JD Advantage positions are found.

This section takes a "generic" approach to describing where in corporate America aspiring JD Advantage job-seeking attorneys should be looking and why.

JD Advantage positions can be found primarily in the following 21 corporate departments/offices:

- Legal/General Counsel
- Board of Directors Staff
- Tax
- Compliance
- Risk Management
- Ethics
- Due Diligence
- Technology Commercialization
- Real Estate
- Litigation Management
- Marketing
- Intellectual Property
- Government Affairs
- Contracting and Procurement
- Acquisitions
- Privacy/Data Protection
- Labor Relations
- Policy Management
- Human Resources
- Diversity
- Training

We'll examine the opportunities in each one of these corporate subdivisions, but first, you need to keep seven things in mind when embarking on this kind of job search:

- **First, different companies organize these legal and law-related functions differently.** A corporation with an *integrated* legal function might combine all of the corporation's legal and law-related responsibilities, including many of the ones specified above, in its General Counsel's Office. At the other extreme, a comparable company in the same industry but with a *differentiated* legal function might have separate departments for each of these functions. Most companies are neither completely integrated nor completely differentiated. Rather, they are likely to be a mix of partially integrated and partially differentiated functions, sometimes with considerable overlap among certain functions. There is typically neither an industry standard nor a company standard regarding corporate structure. A very rough rule of thumb might be: *the larger the company, the more differentiated its legal and law-related functions.* Another rule-of-thumb is that *publicly-traded companies are more likely to have a differentiated legal function than closely-held corporations, the exception being the largest private companies.* If there is a trend in corporate America, it is to separate these functions.

- **Second, job titles for the very same job may vary from one company to another.** What one corporation calls "Privacy" might be called "Cybersecurity" by another and "Data Protection" by a third. When you search for these types of jobs, use the most expansive terminology so that you don't overlook something that might be perfect for you.

- **Third, there is a growing trend toward subdividing certain broad functions** that become "too much" for just one corporate division or office. Compliance is a good example. This function has become so overwhelming and specialized that there are companies today that have broken it down into multiple subspecialties. A multinational corporation, for example, might have separate compliance divisions for each global region in which it does business.

- **Fourth, certain functions are more important in some industries and company types than in others.** For example, healthcare puts a great deal of emphasis on Risk Management for obvious reasons. Biotechnology gives star billing to Technology Commercialization. Litigation Management is prominent in the insurance industry. Compliance is a bigger deal in a public company than in one that is closely-held because publicly-traded firms are more heavily regulated.

- **Fifth, don't expect to find all 21 of these departments/offices in every company.** There are tremendous differences from one company to another. Large companies tend to have more departments and offices with JD Advantage jobs than their smaller counterparts. In addition, certain functions are of greater importance to some industries than others.

- **Sixth, these 21 departments may not be the only places in corporations where attorneys work in JD Advantage jobs.** For example, hospitals, HMOs, and other healthcare provider organizations are trending toward establishing Patient Safety departments and Ombudsmen offices, places where lawyers sometimes play a major role. Moreover, attorneys may also be scattered among various other departments that need daily, on-the-spot legal expertise.

- **Seventh, there will almost always be some overlap among these functional areas.** Any other business model would be irrational and dysfunctional.

The common theme that runs through all of these corporate functions is the added value of hiring attorneys for many of these roles.

Corporate Offices with JD Advantage Jobs

General (In-House) Counsel

Historically, corporate general counsel offices have not had much interest in JD Advantage candidates, not to mention recent law school graduates. That mindset, however, is changing due to the evolution of legal responsibilities as well as the following influences:

- Increased exposure of corporate officers, directors, committees, etc., due to new and more rigorously enforced corporate governance requirements;
- Increased awareness on the part of both management and legal of the valuable business strategy, policy, and planning roles played by attorneys;
- Increased interest in the preventive law role that company attorneys can play if they are conversant with business planning and decision-making;
- Increased appreciation of the potential impact of the legal office on shareholder value;
- Increased interaction with internal clients, including offices with legal or quasi-level responsibilities.

Representative JD Advantage Job Titles

The following is a selection of JD Advantage job titles found in corporate general counsel offices:

- Legal Affairs Coordinator
- Professional Licensing Manager
- Regulatory Specialist
- Legal Knowledge Manager
- Legal Process Outsourcing Manager
- Legal Program Manager
- E-Discovery Specialist

Trends

The number of in-house counsel offices is growing, as is the number of attorney and JD Advantage jobs within them. The larger the company, the more likely it is to have its own general counsel office. However, many smaller companies have joined the movement toward having their own full-time attorneys at an earlier stage in their development than previously.

Bringing legal work traditionally farmed out to outside law firms in-house is trending up as more concern for legal spend and more budget sensitivity is imposed by corporate managers. This is especially the case where another trend can be discerned— having the legal office report directly to the company's Chief Financial Officer.

Publicly-traded companies are more likely to have in-house counsel offices than private firms.

Companies in highly-regulated industry sectors, e.g., Healthcare, Financial Services, Insurance, Pharmaceuticals, Communications, Energy, are also more likely to have in-house counsel offices than those more lightly regulated.

Board of Directors' Staff

Beginning with the enactment of the *Sarbanes-Oxley Act of 2002* in response to the corporate shenanigans of companies like Enron, Tyco, Adelphia, and Worldcom, regulations governing the conduct of corporate boards and accompanying government scrutiny of board activities has exploded, along with lawsuits brought against boards and specific board members by shareholders and others.

Whenever something like this emerges, lawyers are never far behind. Many corporations responded to this by engaging their own attorneys separate from the company in-house counsel staff. In addition, this development "legaled-up" the role of the Corporate Secretary and his or her staff, thus creating a number of JD Advantage jobs that did not exist before.

Representative JD Advantage Job Titles

- Corporate Secretary
- Assistant Corporate Secretary
- Corporate Governance Officer
- Executive Director, Corporate Governance Committee
- Executive Director, Risk Management Committee
- Director of Governance
- Governance Specialist

Trends

Corporate boards are coming under closer government and shareholder scrutiny. In addition, they now must operate in a much higher risk environment than ever before. That signifies that boards will have to continue to expand their independent staffs, including JD Advantage positions.

Tax

Corporate Tax Departments exist primarily for two reasons: (1) To save the company money; and (2) To make certain that the company complies with federal, state and foreign tax laws and regulations. The tax compliance function is as old as the imposition of taxes and has become rather routinized. The more interesting and exciting money-saving function goes far beyond making sure that tax burdens are reduced by taking advantage of all credits, deductions and carryovers to which the corporation is entitled. It also comes into play in virtually every significant corporate transaction, where meticulous tax planning and tax transactional prowess can make or break any deal.

Large companies tend to subdivide the tax compliance function by geography: international, federal, and state and local. Naturally, the more business training and awareness the Tax Department has, the better it can do its tax planning, tax transactional, and tax compliance jobs.

A typical tax management position might have the following responsibilities:

- *Tax Planning*. Identify, develop, analyze, research, implement, and document tax planning initiatives to achieve the lowest sustainable effective tax rate and the lowest cash tax rate for the company. Provide technical tax support to, and team with, the tax audit group in defending planning positions. Work with the compliance group to properly report the tax planning.
- *Tax Advice*. Provide tax advice regarding ongoing business operations and transactions.
- *Mergers and Acquisitions*. Provide tax advice in connection with mergers, acquisitions, joint ventures,

divestitures, and other dispositions. Perform research in connection with mergers, acquisitions, joint ventures and dispositions. Assist in performing due diligence and identifying tax synergies required to value potential targets. Perform research to assist in developing tax-efficient structures for corporate mergers. Assist in drafting the tax-related provisions of transaction agreements and negotiating tax issues with legal counsel for the target, acquirer, or joint venture partner.

Tax department positions sometimes have specialized requirements, such as a JD plus a CPA, LLM in Tax, or a Master's in Taxation.

Representative JD Advantage Job Titles

- Manager, Tax Planning
- M&A Transactions Tax Manager
- Corporate Tax Compliance Manager
- International Tax Compliance Associate

- State and Local Tax Associate
- Tax Analyst
- Tax Associate
- Tax Consultant
- Tax Director
- Tax Manager
- Tax Specialist
- Tax Strategy and Planning Associate

Trends

Tax issues are not going away anytime soon. In fact, globalization, the expansion of multijurisdictional tax liability, and constant tinkering with tax codes by government increase the need for corporate tax expertise. In addition to tax planning requirements, there is also an increasing demand for tax transactional prowess due to the large number of acquisitions and takeovers that mark the global economy.

Compliance

Corporate compliance is nothing new, but has vastly expanded in scope in the 21st century. Compliance encompasses the development, implementation, and monitoring of compliance policies, programs, procedures, and practices applicable to the company's business activities as well as prevention via detection of potential violations of legal and regulatory requirements by the corporation and its employees. Specific compliance programs and policies will vary according to a company's size, location, industry, regulatory regime, operational complexity, and the markets where the company does business.

Compliance has expanded exponentially in recent years and become more specialized, prompted by new federal and state laws and regulations that place substantial additional compliance burdens on many U.S. companies. Chief among these are the following:

- *Health Insurance Portability and Accountability Act of 1996 (HIPAA)*, which established national standards to protect the privacy of personal health information. See also the HIPAA Omnibus Rule.

- *Gramm-Leach-Bliley Financial Modernization Act of 1999,* which protects the privacy of consumer information held by "financial institutions," a term that encompasses a wide variety of organizations not always historically deemed financial services.
- *Public Company Accounting Reform and Investor Protection Act of 2002 (Sarbanes-Oxley),* which established sweeping new or enhanced standards for all U.S. public company boards, management, and public accounting firms.
- *USA Patriot Act,* which increased the ability of law enforcement agencies to search telephone and e-mail communications and medical, financial and other records; eased restrictions on foreign intelligence gathering within the U.S.; and expanded the Secretary of the Treasury's authority to regulate financial transactions, particularly those involving foreign individuals and entities.
- *Affordable Care Act (Obamacare),* the landmark health reform law that placed new regulatory burdens on the healthcare and insurance industries, as well as businesses of all varieties.
- *Wall Street Reform and Consumer Protection (Dodd-Frank) Act,* the largest overhaul of financial services regulation in 70 years.

In large companies, compliance departments may be further divided into multiple units by function or product area.

The compliance function goes far beyond mere regulatory reporting. It often also includes:
- Giving compliance advice.

- Developing compliance policies and procedures.
- Training employees.
- Monitoring regulations and regulatory changes.
- Analyzing new laws and rules for their impact on the company.
- Performing regulatory risk assessments.
- Interacting with regulators.

Opportunities in compliance are growing rapidly. Twenty-first century legislation alone has created thousands of compliance job opportunities.

Compliance duties can vary from one industry to another. Bank compliance officers, for example, may spend much of their time concerned with financial institution regulatory agencies such as the Federal Reserve Board, Comptroller of the Currency, Federal Deposit Insurance Corporation, Consumer Financial Protection Bureau, their state's bank regulatory agency, as well as the Securities and Exchange Commission. Hospital compliance officers may focus their attention on the U.S. Department of Health and Human Services, the state health department, state insurance commission, Center for Medicare and Medicaid Services, and state professional licensing boards.

Representative JD Advantage Job Titles

- Accessibility/Compliance Specialist
- 3rd Party Management Compliance Director
- ADA Compliance Manager
- Advisor, Regulatory Management

- Anti-Bribery Program Manager
- Antitrust Compliance Manager
- Assistant Compliance Officer
- Associate Compliance Officer
- Bank Investment Compliance Officer
- Chief Compliance Officer
- China Compliance Manager
- Claims Legal and Regulatory Compliance Director
- Code of Ethics Compliance Manager
- Commercial Compliance Monitor
- Compliance Analyst
- Compliance Consultant Manager
- Compliance Director
- Compliance Training Officer
- Compliance Trust Officer
- Compliance Manager
- Compliance Manager-Program Assessment
- Compliance Officer
- Compliance Officer (Bank Regulation)
- Compliance Officer (Commercial Banking)
- Compliance Officer (Commodities)
- Compliance Officer (Securities)
- Compliance Representative
- Compliance Program Auditor
- Consumer Lending Compliance Director
- Corporate Compliance Officer/Director
- Corporate Investigations Manager
- Credit/Debit Card Compliance Director
- Customer Care Compliance Manager
- Data Protection Compliance Advisor

- Director/Assistant Vice President – Compliance
- Director, Compliance/Audit
- Director of International Compliance
- Director of State Compliance
- Director of Operational Compliance
- Director, Pharmaceutical Sales & Marketing Compliance
- Director, Sales & Marketing Compliance
- Document Compliance Specialist
- EEO Compliance Manager
- Energy Regulatory Affairs Professional
- Energy Trading Compliance Officer
- Environmental Compliance Manager
- Equal Opportunity Compliance Specialist
- Equities Compliance Officer
- Global Compliance Officer
- Global Trade Compliance Manager
- Grants & Contract Compliance Specialist
- Healthcare Compliance Officer
- Human Resources Compliance Officer
- Immigration Compliance Manager/Officer
- Integrity & Compliance Analyst
- Internet/Web Compliance Manager
- Legal Compliance Officer
- Manager of Compliance and Ethics
- Manager of Export/Import Compliance

- Manager of Global Trading Documentation
- Manager of Regulatory Affairs
- Operational Compliance Manager
- Physician Compliance Officer
- Procurement Analyst, Self Governance/Compliance
- Program Engagement & Assessment Manager
- Program Integrity Specialist
- Regulatory Analyst
- Regulatory Compliance Officer/Director
- Regulatory Impact Analyst
- Regulatory Program Specialist
- Regulatory Implementation Manager
- Research Compliance Officer- Clinical Research
- Research Compliance Officer- Clinical Trials
- Research Compliance Officer- Human Research
- Security Compliance Officer
- Tax Compliance Officer
- Tariff and Regulatory Supervisor
- Telecommunications Regulatory Analyst
- Trucking Compliance Specialist
- Wealth Management Compliance Officer

Trends

The corporate compliance function has grown dramatically in the 21st century, with no slowing down in sight. This is particularly true in sectors such as healthcare and financial services. Other industries are not far behind.

Growing trends in compliance are international compliance and compliance with laws and regulations of foreign countries. As business becomes increasingly global and transborder activities and operations expand, compliance becomes both more complex and more central to business success. Globalization has complicated this function and increased demand for corporate compliance professionals who now must be concerned with compliance requirements in multiple jurisdictions.

For more detailed information about compliance careers, see Volume 2, *Careers in Compliance: JDs Wanted*, in the *21st Century Legal Careers Series*, available in print from http://nalp.org/bookstore or digitally at http://legalcareerview.com.

Due Diligence

Due diligence in this context means the process whereby a potential acquirer or merger partner evaluates a target company or its assets with an eye to an acquisition or merger. JD Advantage jobs abound with respect to such transactions/due diligence positions.

Due diligence involves a very in-depth investigation and analysis of a target company, including:

- Organization and Good Standing
- Financial Information
- Physical Assets
- Real Estate
- Intellectual Property
- Employees and Employee Benefits
- Licenses and Permits
- Environmental Issues
- Taxes
- Material Contracts
- Product and Service Lines
- Customer Information
- Litigation
- Insurance Coverage
- Outside Professionals and Consultants
- Articles and Publicity

Representative JD Advantage Job Titles

- Legal Due Diligence Specialist
- Due Diligence Analyst
- Consultant II, Due Diligence Investigations
- Business Due Diligence Director
- Manager, Transaction Support Services M&A
- Investment Research Director
- Senior Associate – Transaction Advisory Services

Trends

While many companies employ their own staffs to conduct due diligence examinations, there is a growing trend toward engaging outside specialist consulting firms (including law firms and their subsidiaries) to perform these investigations and analyses. There will, nevertheless, always be a role for internal due diligence specialists.

Ethics

Some corporations combine or subsume the Ethics function with Compliance and/or Risk Management. However, an increasing number differentiate all three functions.

In recent years, corporate ethics has become much more important due to two very significant U.S. government initiatives: The *Sarbanes-Oxley Act* and the *Organizational Sentencing Guidelines* issued by the U.S. Sentencing Commission (http://www.ussc.gov. *Sarbanes-Oxley* imposes stringent compliance requirements on companies, which in turn requires heightened ethics awareness among virtually all company employees. The *Organizational Sentencing Guidelines* impose heavy fines for corporate ethics violations, as well as potential jail time for corporate executives.

Typical Corporate Ethics Department responsibilities include:

- Serving as the ethics adviser to senior corporate officers and employees.
- Rendering both written and oral opinions or interpretations on the ethical implications of policy matters and proposed corporate activities.
- Participating in high-level planning and policy deliberations.
- Implementing corporate ethics policies and codes of conduct.
- Serving as an expert on matters of standards of conduct and advising employees on these matters.

- Administering and processing financial disclosure reports, and reviewing outside activities, honorary degrees, official duty activity, and awards.
- Maintaining currency in the field through independent study and research.
- Identifying systemic trends in the company and representing it before internal and external committees and organizations.
- Leading and overseeing policy development, benchmarking and regulatory review.
- Managing the development and implementation of new communication and training initiatives (including the design of Internet-based training to assess employees) to targeted employee groups regarding integrity, ethical decision-making, and the requirements of codes of conduct and related policies.
- Analyzing off-shoring and business acquisition issues involving application of the codes of conduct and ethics policies and procedures to new regions and entities.
- Recommending specific changes to policies based on the particular region or acquisition and independently managing the implementation of the recommendations.
- Writing educational materials regarding recommendations and giving presentations to affected employees to communicate policy decisions.
- Resolving high-profile ethics issues and evaluating requests for exceptions to ethics policies.
- Reviewing and approving outside activity requests by employees.

Representative JD Advantage Job Titles

- Legal Ethics and Compliance Counsel (International)
- Legal Director – Corporate Governance and Ethics
- Ethics Compliance Counsel, Business Objects
- Director, Corporate Office of Ethics and Compliance
- Senior Manager, Compliance and Ethics
- Ethics Manager – National Compliance
- Ethics Program Manager
- Ethics and Compliance Investigations Manager
- Director, Ethics Policy
- Vice President of Ethics and Compliance
- Ethics Case Manager
- Associate Ethics Director
- Hospital Executive Ethics Officer
- Ethics Leader, Training,
- Director of Ethics

Trends

The *Organizational Sentencing Guidelines* spurred the growth of corporate ethics departments in the 1990s. However, when it became apparent that investigations and prosecutions of alleged corporate ethics violations were not going to flood the courts, the movement waned. Then, the constant refrain of corporate wrongdoing prompted by the Enron debacle and other corporate scandals re-energized the business ethics movement. The *Sarbanes-Oxley Act of 2002* followed eight years later by the *Dodd-Frank Act* gave considerable impetus to this movement and it is still prospering today. Given the uncertainty associated with Republican control of both ends of

Pennsylvania Avenue, it is difficult to predict whether the corporate ethics function will continue its robust pace.

Risk Management

Corporate Risk Management departments have proliferated widely and in terms of responsibilities in recent years, as company risks, exposures, and threats have multiplied and become more challenging. Risk managers have a very bright future in corporate America. At the same time, compensation for risk managers has improved considerably as their importance to the company bottom line becomes more obvious. In some organizations, there may be some overlap with either or both of the Compliance and Ethics functions.

Typical corporate Risk Manager duties include:

- Identifying, preventing and managing risk, including strategic planning, oversight of risk management projects, risk management interventions, and legal and technical advice.
- Creating a culture of compliance, ethics and integrity.
- Maintaining knowledge of and assuring compliance with organizational rules, codes of conduct, policies and procedures, and applicable regulatory requirements and accreditation standards.
- Responding to observed, reported, and possible fraud or abuse.
- Planning, directing and providing risk management education.

- Providing timely risk management counsel to company officers and staff on potential risk management issues.
- Investigating and managing claims, suits and litigation processes.
- Dealing with insurance claim adjusters and outside counsel on lawsuits.
- Handling subpoenas and attorney letters.
- Recommending process improvements to minimize risk.
- Monitoring changes in the law affecting the business and developing policy language to assure compliance.

Representative JD Advantage Job Titles

- Clinical Risk Specialist
- Contract Risk Manager
- Country Risk Analyst
- Crisis Manager
- Director of Risk Management
- Hospital Risk Manager
- Insurance Manager – Risk
- Legal Risk Manager
- Manager, Corporate Risk Management/Insurance
- Recovery Manager
- Risk Analyst
- Risk and Compliance Subject-Matter Expert
- Risk and Patient Safety Director
- Risk Management Consultant
- Risk Manager
- Senior Advisor, Risk Management
- Trust Risk Analyst

Trends

Corporate risk managers are rapidly rising in esteem and correspondingly in compensation as their value to their employers becomes more apparent. Risk management is probably as close as it is possible to come to being deemed indispensable. Moreover, the frequent combination of risk management and compliance makes risk managers even more central to their organizations' viability and success.

The major corporate employers of risk managers are healthcare companies, especially provider organizations, and financial services companies, but the profession is spreading into other industry sectors.

For more detailed information about risk management careers, see Volume 6, *Risk Management: The Indispensable Profession*, in the *21st Century Legal Careers Series*, available in print from http://nalp.org/bookstore or digitally at http://legalcareerview.com.

Technology Licensing/Commercialization

The value of attorneys to the technology commercialization function is both obvious and central to success. They have the training and facility with the tools needed to assess the state of legal protection and, in many instances, the commercial viability of potential acquisitions and licenses, and can provide the requisite knowledge of intellectual property (IP) and contract negotiation to the process.

Typical corporate Technology Commercialization duties include:

- Searching for and identifying new reliable sources of technology innovation.
- Evaluating the commercial viability of potential technology to be acquired.
- Reviewing, drafting, and negotiating technology agreements and licenses.
- Drafting and negotiating complex technology contracts, as well as professional service agreements.
- Analyzing, modifying and proposing contract terms and conditions to determine conformity with company policy.
- Advising senior management on technology licensing and intellectual property issues.
- Supporting the improvement of the company's legal processes and form agreements.
- Managing legal disputes.
- Providing legal compliance training.
- Participating in other corporate transactional matters.
- Tracking and maintaining technology licenses.
- Developing a legal strategy for technology-centered transactions based upon the technical and business needs of the company.
- Working with outside counsel to draft and negotiate software licenses, patent licenses, IP-core licenses, statements of work, and development agreements.

- Providing legal support for departments in need of technology counsel, including international sourcing and outsourcing.
- Staying current with knowledge and trends within the industry.
- Developing and maintaining vendor relationships.

Representative JD Advantage Job Titles

- Associate Director – Licensing
- Business Development Manager, Licensing Programs
- Director, Customer and Partner Licensing
- Director, Licensing and Business Development
- Director, Licensing and Compliance
- Franchise Licensing Manager
- Healthcare Licensing Manager
- IP Commercialization Specialist
- IP Licensing Specialist – Military Products & Services
- Legal Support Specialist, Trademark and Copyright Group
- Licensing Consultant
- Licensing Manager
- Licensing Specialist
- Media Licensing Officer
- Software Licensing Manager
- Technical Licensing Manager
- Technology Acquisition & Licensing Consultant
- Technology/Outsourcing/Licensing Transactions Specialist
- Technology Sourcing Manager
- Technology Transfer Specialist

Trends

Twenty-five years ago, the mix of corporate assets was approximately 80-20 in favor of tangible goods. Today, it has flipped to 80-20 IP and intangible assets. Technology commercialization has consequently become a very important source of new products and business growth for many companies and thus, a major contributor to both the bottom line and shareholder value. This function is comprised of two distinct roles in many corporations: (1) Securing new technologies that can be commercially exploited; and (2) Licensing corporate technology assets to other organizations. Many companies combine both roles in one department. However, there are also a large number of corporations that still keep them separate, in which case technology acquisitions are usually handled by either the IP Department or the Acquisitions/Transactions function.

For more detailed information about technology commercialization careers, see Volume 5, *"Soft" Intellectual Property Law: IP Opportunities for Non-STEM Attorneys*, in the *21st Century Legal Careers Series*, available in print from http://nalp.org/bookstore or digitally at http://legalcareerview.com.

Intellectual Property

Corporate IP departments are growing in importance as companies realize the value of their intellectual assets and the need to protect them both in this country and abroad.

Attorneys are attractive to IP departments, depending on the scope of responsibilities vested in them. In some companies, the IP function may also encompass the technology commercialization and licensing functions.

Typical IP Department duties include:

- Planning and implementing anti-counterfeiting strategies in different countries, including customs seizures as well as all available criminal and civil remedies.
- Advising clients regarding the protection of IP, negotiating and drafting agreements regarding IP rights, and ancillary responsibilities related to marketing, promotions and advertising agreements.
- Managing the monitoring and enforcement of products in world markets to help ensure that genuine products reach company customers through authorized channels at company-determined prices.
- Leading global brand protection market monitoring and enforcement operations.
- Prosecuting patents, trademarks and copyrights.
- Contributing to the review, drafting and negotiating of product or licensing agreements to ensure the effective acquisition and licensing of IP rights.
- Managing and overseeing the company's trademark portfolio and enforcement work.
- Refining existing strategies and developing new strategies for brand protection in relation to new brands, business models and markets.

- Negotiating resolutions of registry conflicts, and preparing settlement or co-existence agreements to protect the company's rights.
- Coordinating brand/IP matters in connection with international expansion.

*Note: Many IP department positions **do not** require a science or engineering background or admission to the Patent Bar.*

Representative JD Advantage Job Titles

- Chief IP Officer
- Chief of Content Protection
- Chief Strategy Officer
- Content Protection Officer
- Corporate Copyright Specialist
- Foreign Filing Specialist
- Intellectual Asset Manager
- IP Director/Manager
- IP Policy Specialist
- IP Resources Director
- IP Rights Enforcement Officer
- IP Strategist
- Patent Administrator
- Patent Analyst
- Rights Manager
- Technology Manager – IP
- Trademark Legal Manager

Trends

High technology companies lead the way when it comes to discrete IP departments. However, other companies that own a large number of IP assets also have them. As IP looms larger in corporate financial statements, this function is destined to continue its impressive growth.

For more detailed information about IP careers, see Volume 5, *"Soft" Intellectual Property Law: IP Opportunities for Non-STEM Attorneys*, in the *21st Century Legal Careers Series*, available from in print http://www.nalp.org/bookstore or digitally at http://legalcareerview.com.

Real Estate

Corporate Real Estate departments are primarily responsible for real estate transactional matters, including acquisitions, financing, divestitures, leases, etc., as well as property management. Depending on the employer's industry, the Real Estate department's responsibilities may vary considerably.

Real Estate department responsibilities combine legal knowledge with business acumen in order to select the right properties at the right price, acquire and manage them, and dispose of them.

Typical Real Estate department duties include:

- Managing acquisition analysis and due diligence.
- Directing site acquisition processes.
- Negotiating real estate and leasing contracts.
- Developing and standardizing rules and procedures.
- Drafting and reviewing sales contracts/listing contracts, leases, etc.

- Implementing real estate legal and disclosure requirements.
- Advising the company on real estate issues.
- Assisting with management of litigation and threatened litigation.
- Participating in the negotiation of settlements.
- Dealing with property owners, governmental authorities and neighbors in connection with real estate and legal issues relating to real estate development and other corporate real estate.
- Managing escrow activities.
- Reviewing title commitments, surveys, and closing documentation.
- Negotiating easements.
- Preparing platting documents.
- Reviewing and implementing building listing agreements.

Representative JD Advantage Job Titles

- Development Specialist
- Director of Real Estate
- Land Acquisition Manager
- Lease Administrator
- Lease Negotiator
- Real Estate Development Coordinator
- Real Estate Deal Manager
- Real Estate Manager
- Real Estate Portfolio Manager
- Real Estate Specialist—Acquisition
- Real Estate Specialist—Litigation
- Real Estate Strategist

- Transmission Right-of-Way Specialist

Trends

The major employers or corporate real estate professionals are hospitality and recreation companies, retailers, real estate developers, franchisors, and telecommunications firms. As those industries and firms go, so go JD Advantage jobs in corporate real estate departments.

Litigation Management

Litigation Management, historically the province of the corporate general counsel's office, has been separated out in many companies – particularly those burdened with a large number of lawsuits. This business model predominates in the insurance industry.

Attorneys are an asset to Litigation Management departments because they not only understand the nuances of litigation, but they also know how to evaluate the costs and benefits of litigating vs. settling a case as well as how to bring management principles to bear on legal fee and performance auditing.

As a rule, litigation managers require several years of involvement with litigation, but subordinate positions sometimes do not.

Typical Litigation Management department duties include:

- Overall management of lawsuits against the company.
- Selecting outside counsel.
- Directing retained outside counsel.
- Participating in strategizing litigation.
- Managing the course of litigation to minimize legal costs and exposures.
- Monitoring outside counsel performance.
- Auditing and assessing the billing practices, fees, litigation performance and guideline compliance by the company's outside counsel.
- Reviewing, evaluating, negotiating and settling non-litigated matters and claims against the company.
- Working with company insurers on successful resolution of covered claims and lawsuits.
- Preparing legal documents related to claims (releases, stipulations, etc.).
- Advising management as to best practices and avoidance of professional liability exposures, and drafting of corporate policies to accomplish this.
- Reviewing marketing materials and internal documents to avoid legal exposures.
- Collecting and analyzing data pertaining to company case handling and management.
- Developing and maintaining litigation management tools.
- Assisting outside counsel in trial preparation support activity, including case staffing, witness preparation and other activities

Representative JD Advantage Job Titles

- Case Assessment Consultant
- Chief Discovery Officer
- Compliance – Litigation Manager
- Director of Complex Case Support
- Legal Bill Review Auditor
- Legal Strategy Officer
- Litigation Analyst
- Litigation Management Team Manager
- Litigation Management Trainer
- Litigation Manager
- Litigation Support Consultant/Specialist
- Litigation Support Project Manager
- Regional Litigation Management Specialist

Trends

We live in both the most highly litigious society on the planet as well as the country that generates by far the most litigation *per capita* (The Trump Organization has sued or been sued every two-and-one-half days for the past 30+ years!) Litigation management is a rapidly maturing field. Every company of significant size has at least one person tasked with this role.

Marketing

Marketing may seem like an unusual place to find attorneys. However, Marketing departments in many major companies now have their own attorneys practicing both mainstream law and serving in JD Advantage jobs. This is particularly the case in companies that develop and sell investment products and in industries where labeling and product information are subject to heightened regulatory scrutiny, as well as the risk of liability exposure.

Typical Marketing department duties include:

- Advising on all aspects of advertising and marketing law.
- Supporting direct advertising sales and marketing teams, advising them about consumer laws related to direct sales, advertising, media publishing, pricing and delivery.
- Developing policy for the marketing of company products and services.
- Reviewing advertising and marketing communications for legal compliance and product consistency.
- Negotiating, drafting, and reviewing sales agent agreements, marketing and affinity partner agreements, customer agreements, promotion and sponsorship agreements, and vendor agreements for various sales channels.
- Developing business cases, marketing plans, coordination of new product implementation, product launch, and product and program evaluation for the appropriate market segments with due consideration of the legal and liability implications of same.
- Performing brand search trademark screening.
- Developing and leading initiatives aimed at prevention of grey marketing, counterfeiting, and related business risks.

- Educating and training the sales force on company policies.
- Providing legal advice to promotional and regulatory departments and brand development teams on media communications, labeling, strategy, issues management, competitor issues, product claims litigation, alliance management, external environment, and client education.
- Drafting and negotiating advertising and media agreements, online sales agreements, co-marketing agreements, confidentiality agreements and, agreements for content licensing.

Representative JD Advantage Job Titles

- Director – Marketing Business Development
- Marketing Support Supervisor
- Legal Database Marketer
- Market Development Associate
- Legal Product Sales Consultant
- Advanced Markets Senior Sales Consultant
- Advanced Insurance Sales Consultant
- Manager – Health Care Consulting Practice
- Legal Solutions Consultant
- Product Marketing Manager

Trends

Job growth in this realm is directly proportional to the growth in advertising media available to companies. Until recently, the principal employers of attorneys in JD Advantage positions in corporate Marketing departments had been financial services firms. These jobs can now be found in a variety of other industries.

Government Affairs

Government Affairs demands multidisciplinary skills that often include a legal background, as well as marketing, management, communication, and very strong interpersonal skills. Once these skills are embedded, they are eminently transferable to a variety of different venues.

Typical Government Affairs responsibilities include:

- Managing corporate government affairs activities, focusing on Congress, state legislatures, governors' offices, and other departments and agencies.
- Representing the company before federal and state officials, legislatures, and industry/business organizations.
- Managing the legislative agenda, including reviewing bills for potential impact on company business, developing positions with internal business units and subject-matter experts, and communicating views to appropriate committees and other officials.
- Managing contract lobbyists in the states.
- Organizing coalition activities with other companies in the industry, and with consumer groups, to advance the company's agenda.
- Working with attorneys handling company regulatory issues to gain political support.

- Managing the company's political program, including use of corporate and PAC contributions where appropriate.
- Participating in federal and state administrative proceedings.
- Formulating policy positions on key issues with the Congress, state legislatures, the administration and other federal agencies.
- Developing and implementing strategic plans on key policy positions.
- Monitoring and analyzing key legislative and regulatory proposals that affect the industry and assess their impact on the company.
- Developing relationships with key regulators, legislators, and policymakers.
- Developing activities to position the company as a thought leader in industry policy.
- Preparing policy briefings for internal executives and business units.
- Representing the company at trade associations and industry coalitions.
- Interacting with other companies/thought leaders on key issues.
- Managing outside legal and lobbying resources.

Representative JD Advantage Job Titles

- Manager – Government Relations
- Government Affairs Professional
- Lobbyist
- Government Affairs Manager
- Public Policy Analyst
- Legislative Director

- Government
  Business
  Development
  Manager
- Government Liaison
- Public Affairs
  Government
  Relations Associate

Trends

More than 13,000 trade and professional associations are present in the Washington, DC metropolitan area. Their core mission is all about government relations. Over 375 of the Fortune 500 companies have in-house government relations personnel representing them in Washington, DC. A lot of this is replicated in state capitals. Major state capitals, such as Sacramento, Austin, Tallahassee, and Albany, also have large numbers of government relations professionals. The Supreme Court's "liberation" of corporate money for political campaigns has contributed to the growth of this profession.

Procurement

Corporate procurement offices are staffed with a significant number of lawyers, for the obvious reason that there is a great deal of contract law involved in the procurement process. Another not so obvious reason has to do with the other side of the transaction—when the company is the seller, especially to the U.S. government. In a typical year, 275,000 companies sell goods or services to the government and deal directly with its 35,000 contracting officers, of which at least 7,000 are attorneys.

Typical Procurement Department duties include:

- Sourcing spending categories.
- Industry analysis to identify size of industry, leading players, and specific industry characteristics.
- Developing contracts with new suppliers or renegotiating existing contracts.
- Managing the contract negotiation process by: defining the negotiation strategy; leading the sourcing process for new and expiring contracts; and identifying opportunities for expanded supplier relationships to enable enhanced business partnerships.
- Identifying metrics to evaluate supplier performance and achieve the best value.
- Developing close relationships with both suppliers and appropriate client groups.
- Analyzing, interpreting, and providing oversight on company procurement actions or adherence to company policies and procedures, procurement terms and conditions, government and company directives, law and regulations.
- Conducting self-governance internal audits to identify problems and trends and recommend improvements while guiding corrective actions.

Representative JD Advantage Job Titles

- Category Manager
- Contract Agent
- Contract Administrator
- Contract & Rights Manager
- Contract Manager
- Contract Negotiator
- Contract Specialist

- Director, Contracts & Procurement
- Energy Procurement Manager
- Manager, Contracts Due Diligence
- Manager – Strategic Procurement
- Procurement Analyst
- Procurement Manager
- Procurement/Materials Director
- Procurement Specialist

Trends

The contract and procurement function is ubiquitous and is found across all business sectors and industries. It is also "trickling down" as more small companies sell their products and source materials and services worldwide.

Acquisitions

In some companies, the Acquisitions function has become a specialty. Typically, this is a discrete function in large companies that are always on the hunt for new markets and revenue streams and centers. The Fortune 500 corporation that bought my company, for example, bought more than 20 other companies in the same calendar year.

Some companies subsume Due Diligence under Acquisitions, but that is becoming increasingly rare because due diligence these days encompasses more than analyzing the worth and worthiness of target firms. It also includes examining prospective vendors.

Typical Acquisitions Department responsibilities include:

- Identifying potential target companies and merger partners.
- Projecting how the transaction will affect the acquiring company.
- Determining the financial impact of a merger or acquisition.
- Developing the merger or acquisition strategy.
- Organizing and negotiating deals.
- Participating in the due diligence process.
- Finalizing deals.
- Managing the actual acquisition or merger.

Representative JD Advantage Job Titles

- Acquisitions Specialist/Manager
- Mergers and Acquisitions Specialist
- Acquisitions/Divestiture Professional
- Acquisitions Agent

Trends

Generally, M & A "mania" closely follows the business cycle. During the Great Recession, for example, the Fortune 500 company that bought my firm went from buying more than 20 companies in a single year to buying just one the next year, which was the first year of the downturn. However, since the economy began growing again, activity has picked up far beyond what could have been anticipated based on past economic cycles. That is due in large part to two factors: (1) the pace of technological innovation, and (2) the impact of globalization on corporate strategic planning. The fear of being left behind by either or both factors is prompting a surge in M & A activity worldwide.

Another important trend is the "professionalization" of the corporate acquisitions role. JDs with a business, economics, finance, or accounting education (undergraduate major or graduate degree) or background are in the best position to compete for these jobs. In addition, strong analytical and communication skills are valued highly.

Labor Relations

Labor relations is still a viable career for attorneys seeking opportunities outside of traditional law practice, despite the gut-wrenching tumult that both public and private sector unions have endured in the last generation. However, both historical trends, restrictive state legislation (especially right-to-work laws), and the transformation of the global economy, as well as ideological shifts, make it imperative that anyone contemplating a labor relations career pick his or her spots very carefully and only after extensive due diligence and sensitivity to industry developments.

Organized labor is under siege. That is not news, and also not new. In times of societal economic distress, labor is always under pressure. Liberal collective bargaining agreements (CBAs) are a product of annual GDP growth rates averaging just over 3 percent over a term of years. This was the average economic growth achieved by the United States for 60+ years, until the advent of the Great Recession.

However, the pressures on organized labor today are much more profound than ever before because of the technology and globalization overlays, supplemented by political assaults. The contraction of the world and the merging of national economies make it easier than ever for companies, even small ones, to go where labor is cheap. And cheap labor is a synonym for non-union labor. Add to that the fact that more than half of the states now have enacted right-to-work laws, including such former bastions of organized labor as Ohio, Michigan, and Indiana, along with the disappearance of the New Deal coalition that was the bedrock of the Democratic Party for two generations before it abandoned labor and gravitated toward a "meritocratic" base.

What all of this means for legal and law-related employment is fewer opportunities on both sides of the employer-employee divide. That does not mean that there are no jobs or possible labor relations careers out there, just that you have to be more careful in doing your due diligence and picking your spots. That includes assessing where your prospective employer is likely to be down the road.

The plummet in private sector union membership to below 7 percent today means that both unions and employers have fewer labor attorney and law-related positions to offer. That decline is likely to continue. The "trickle over" effect to private sector unions from the public sector union protests in Wisconsin in 2011 and 2012, and Governor Scott Walker's survival of a recall election in that state, harmed private sector unions even more. Union leaders allowed hubris and a terrible misreading of the public mood to cause them to overreach. In the process, they may have harmed the labor movement irreparably.

This bleak picture does not mean that there are no labor relations jobs for JDs. There are, but they are concentrated in select locations: the Northeast, California and the upper Midwest. The "bluer" the state, the more job opportunities you are likely to find. Organized labor, for example, still comprises 25 percent of the workforce in New York State.

Representative JD Advantage Job Titles

- Industrial Relations Specialist
- HR Manager – Labor Relations
- Labor Negotiator/Mediator
- Labor Relations Consultant
- Labor Relations Manager/Specialist/ Analyst
- Labor Relations Planning & Analysis Manager

Trends

Both parties to private sector collective bargaining are hiring fewer labor relations professionals, but for different reasons. Management no longer needs a large cadre of labor relations professionals because labor actions—including strikes and work slowdowns—are no longer as frequent or threatening as they were in the past. Labor unions no longer have the same level of financial resources necessary to engage a similar size cadre.

The pendulum has clearly swung against unions and is still swinging to the right. The key determinant of whether organized labor will survive and continue to play a significant role in the American workplace is the economy. If the economy keeps limping along at modest growth rates, this is not going to be a good era for unions or for any growth in labor law-related employment opportunities. However, if manufacturing "reshores" from places like China and Mexico, you can expect more labor relations job opportunities. Just don't expect a flood.

Policy Management

As business becomes more complex and subject to both more and new threats, an increasing number of which are existential, many businesses have seen the need to better coordinate overall corporate policy and have established Policy Management offices to that end.

Note that there will invariably be considerable overlap between such an office and Compliance, Risk Management, Ethics, and other functions described in this booklet.

Policy Management offices are charged with overall development, supervision, and administration of both company-wide and specific departmental policies. Because so much of corporate activity is infused with law, it is inevitable that sophisticated companies with foresight engage attorneys to participate in policy development and application.

Policy Management office duties include:

- Formulating corporate policies.
- Drafting policy documents.
- Prioritizing policy and document development.
- Distributing policies and supporting documentation.
- Assessing policy process and policy application.
- Updating policies.

Representative JD Advantage Job Titles

- Policy Development Specialist
- Director of Policy Development
- Policy Analyst
- Policy Writer
- Intellectual Property Policy Officer
- Policy Advisor
- Cyber Policy Analyst

Trends

Policy management is a growth arena in corporate America, one that is likely to continue to expand as business becomes a more complex and competitive milieu and requires more attention to long-range strategic planning.

Human Resources

Over the past several decades, the corporate Human Resources (HR) function has vastly increased in scope, depth, and importance, mainly as a result of a spate of federal and state legislation that expanded inclusion and more closely scrutinized equal employment opportunity and regulatory compliance requirements. Consequently, this drove HR departments to hire their own attorneys for both mainstream legal and JD Advantage positions. In fact, a growing number of HR offices in companies of all sizes are now headed by individuals with a law degree.

Today's corporate HR offices are charged with a wide range of duties, including:

- Sourcing and hiring employees
- Promotions
- Reassignments
- Terminations
- Compensation and payroll
- Handling and explaining benefits (including same-sex benefits)
- Equal employment opportunity
- Workplace safety
- Employee manuals
- Certain aspects of training
- Professional development
- Position classification and grading
- Salary determination
- Performance appraisal review and processing
- Awards review and processing
- Personnel data entry and records maintenance
- Work Permitting Immigration Visa Program
- Employee assistance referral
- Workers' compensation
- Regulatory compliance

- Hiring of immigrants
- The Affordable Care Act
- Unemployment compensation

A bit more elaboration on some of these responsibilities is in order.

- Recruiting and hiring are fraught with sensitive legal issues, including: creating legally effective job descriptions; writing job offers and rejection documents that deter lawsuits; obtaining information on applicants via references, examination of social media accounts, and criminal background checks; and drafting employment contracts.

- Workplace privacy and employee monitoring, including: searches of desks, smartphones, etc.; monitoring workplace communications and computer use; workplace investigations; and employee surveillance, has become a core function.

- Drafting sound and defensible employee handbooks, including: disclaimers; employee classifications; what laws, regulations, and policies to include; and social media policies, is more important than ever.

- Wage and benefits matters, including: governing laws; navigating Fair Labor Standards Act requirements; overtime considerations; wage and hour "traps," and handling part-time, temporary, intermittent, and intern employees have become more disputatious.

- Leave, including: the Family and Medical Leave Act; handling military leave; and creating and administering leave policies, have become major corporate HR office issues.

- Discrimination and harassment, including: managing complaints; recordkeeping; and prevention, are always sensitive matters.

- Discipline and termination, including: policy development; determining when to discharge; using employee evaluations to minimize liability when discharging employees; and drafting discharge letters, waivers, and releases, are dangerous waters.

Representative JD Advantage Job Titles

- Employee Benefit Plan Specialist
- Employee Disability Programs Manager
- Employee Relations Manager/Specialist
- Employment and Training Specialist
- Equal Opportunity Compliance Specialist
- Human Resources Compliance Officer
- Human Resources Director
- Retirement Systems Administrator
- Salary Administration Specialist
- Affirmative Action/EEO Officer
- Cultural Diversity Director
- EEO Manager/Officer

- Equity Coordinator

Trends

The trend toward hiring attorneys to serve in top–level HR positions will continue because the legal aspects of HR are not going to diminish or disappear. Moreover, the natural tendency is for attorney HR directors to favor placing attorneys in subordinate roles in the HR office.

Diversity

This is a fairly new corporate departmental discipline that has been prompted by both societal changes in attitude, law, and regulation as well as by the need to ascertain and assure companies that their vendors, including prospective outside counsel, have active equal employment opportunity policies in place. In fact, much of what has occurred in the diversity arena among Fortune 1,000 companies has been generated by their scrutiny of law firm diversity policies and programs.

Representative JD Advantage Job Titles

- Diversity Management Director
- Cultural Diversity Director
- Multicultural Initiatives Director
- Director of Diversity and Inclusion
- Director of Diversity, Equity & Inclusion
- Diversity Researcher
- Diversity Coordinator

- Diversity Recruiting Program Manager
- Workforce Development Manager

Trends

In the past, corporations tended to include the diversity function under their HR office, if then. The trend today and for the last decade or so has been to separate out the function and place it in its own department. *Caveat: At this writing and with a new administration in power in Washington, DC, it is impossible to predict if this trend will continue.*

Training

Corporate training has expanded tremendously in the last two decades in lockstep with the ramping up of government scrutiny of corporate activities. Consequently, what was heretofore a relatively secondary activity posited for the most part in the HR office has now evolved into a major corporate concern pervading many departments, offices and matters. Corporate training responsibilities today encompass virtually all of the departments and offices described in this booklet. The result is both more formalized training programs and a move by many companies to place the entire training responsibility in a separate corporate department.

Corporations undertake a great deal of legal and law-related training, prompted by the *U.S. Sentencing Commission's Organizational Sentencing Guidelines* (http://www.ussc.gov), as well as by the compliance mandates of *HIPAA*, the *Financial*

Modernization Act of 1999 (Gramm-Leach-Bliley Act), Sarbanes-Oxley Act of 2002, Dodd-Frank Act, Affordable Care Act, and a host of other federal and state laws and regulations. The primary topical areas that receive the most focus from a training perspective are ethics, compliance, data protection, risk management, and diversity.

The new emphasis on training has also opened up opportunities for specialty consulting firms and law firm training subsidiaries. This is probably the corporate arena most conducive to the engagement of outside services.

Corporate consulting subsidiaries of law firms are a relatively new phenomenon and are proliferating throughout the legal community. The impetus behind such businesses is both financial and defensive. Financial because law firms can earn additional revenue from existing clients, as well as attract new clients, by offering additional services. Defensive because management consulting firms now offer "thinly-veiled" legal services to their clients and are perceived as a serious threat by law firms.

"Ancillary business" is the term of choice describing these ventures, a term devised to ward off scrutiny by bar regulators concerned about the impact of such initiatives on client confidentiality and proscriptions on revenue-sharing by lawyers and non-lawyers.

Subsidiaries are usually creatures of the larger law firms. The key point, however, is that attorneys can often compete for these positions without being filtered out by virtue of where they went to law school or where (or if) they are admitted to the bar. Candidates who also bring the added value of a dual career to the table are also very competitive. The traditional hiring standards that apply to new associates and lateral attorneys generally are not applied to candidates for subsidiary positions.

One of the hottest arenas into which law firm subsidiaries have ventured is legal and law-related training. A lot of subsidiary training offerings have to do with the multitude of legal ramifications generated by HR functions and decisions.

Representative JD Advantage Job Titles

- Compliance Training Officer
- Training Professional
- Employment and Training Specialist
- Legal Training Coordinator

Trends

Look for the training function to continue to expand. The business world is not getting any less complex, and the risks of employee "glitches" have escalated by orders of magnitude.

A Look at JD Advantage–Heavy Industries

Two industries offer a very large number of JD Advantage jobs. Let's take a quick look at them.

Financial Services

Banks, thrifts, credit unions, insurance companies, securities brokerages, and other financial services institutions employ a great many attorneys in JD Advantage positions.

Four major legislative developments have transformed the financial services industry in the 21st century and kindled dramatic law-related job creation:

- **Financial Modernization Services (Gramm-Leach-Bliley) Act of 1999.** This law partially deregulated the financial services industry, (foolishly) eliminating the Glass-Steagall firewall that separated commercial banking from investment banking and that had served the national economy so well since the Great Depression. What proved bad for the country was very beneficial to attorneys seeking both mainstream and JD Advantage jobs.

- **Public Company Accounting Reform and Investor Protection (Sarbanes-Oxley) Act of 2002.** The excesses of Enron and its ilk led to this first foray into financial services "re-regulation." Industry corporate governance and compliance requirements exploded and created demand for compliance, governance, and other professionals, many of whom came from the legal profession.

- **Wall Street Reform and Consumer Protection (Dodd-Frank) Act of 2010**. This law, Congress' direct response to the shenanigans and worse that caused the financial services industry and greater economy meltdowns of 2008-2009, is still being implemented. Its 2,300 pages of poorly written law and 398 statutorily mandated regulations vastly expanded the need for compliance professionals, risk managers, and other JD Advantage professionals. *Caveat: This law and its bevy of regulations may be under siege under the Trump administration and Republican Congress.*

- **Recent Bank Secrecy Act Amendments**. A series of enactments have expanded the basic *Bank Secrecy Act's* ability to go after fraud and questionable transactions while extending the law's reach into additional economic sectors that, broadly interpreted, also constitute financial services. Both enforcers and defenders of alleged defrauders have benefited, career-wise, from these amendments.

To summarize, whether regulating or deregulating, the impact on JD Advantage job opportunities is a net positive.

Financial services is a vast and increasingly complicated industry comprised of tens of thousands of private sector organizations (banks and insurance companies being the most numerous). JD Advantage jobs are generated largely in response to the 18 U.S. government agencies and 10+ Self-Regulatory Organizations that regulate the industry.

The industry has gone global like no other, as evidenced by the accepted (and unfortunate) fact that, if Greece or Cyprus suffer a hiccup, Europe catches pneumonia and the U.S. comes away with, at a minimum, a very bad cold. In addition to the many multinational companies and international banks, insurers, etc., there are also an increasing number of international organizations that have a stake in monitoring, enforcing and attempting to control and mitigate economic disruptions caused by the industry.

Financial Services Law-Related Job Titles

The following law-related job titles mesh well with a law degree and are often populated by attorneys.

Selected Job Titles

- Advanced Insurance Marketing Consultant
- Bank International Trade Specialist
- Bank Investment Compliance Officer
- Bank Probate Administrator/ Officer
- Benefits Professional
- Capital Market Consultant
- Carbon Transactions Manager
- Claims Director
- Claims/Settlement/Termination Specialist
- Commercial Lending Manager

- Community Reinvestment Act Director
- Compliance Manager
- Compliance Officer (Bank Regulation)
- Compliance Officer (Commercial Banking)
- Compliance Officer (Commodities)
- Compliance Officer (Securities)
- Compliance Representative
- Compliance Trust Officer
- Conflicts of Interest Oversight Officer
- Consumer Credit Specialist
- Consumer Response Specialist
- Corporate Finance Executive
- Credit Examiner
- Due Diligence Manager
- Employee Benefits Trust Administrator
- Equities Compliance Officer
- Escrow Agent
- Estate/Fiduciary Administrator
- Estate Planner
- Financial Advisor
- Financial Analyst-High-Net-Worth
- Financial Planner
- Financial Risks Claims Supervisor
- Financial Services Analyst
- Financial Services Sales Agent
- Fraud Risks & Controls Manager/Senior Manager/Director
- Industry Specialist
- Institutional Sales Officer
- Investment Banking Associate/Officer
- Large Loss Claims Consultant
- Legal Advertising/Sales Literature Manager

- Legal Fee Auditor/Legal Cost Specialist
- Legal Investment Analyst
- Legal Product Manager-Corporate
- Legal Product Manager-Private Label Funds
- Legal Product Manager-Securities/Brokerage
- Loan Administrator/Specialist
- Loan Workout Officer
- Mergers and Acquisitions Specialist
- Mutual Fund Administrator
- Public Finance Consultant
- Regulatory Control Officer
- Securities Firm Executive
- Securities Transactions Analyst
- Transactions Associate/Manager
- Trust Advisor/Officer/Administrator/Executive
- Trust Benefits Specialist
- Trust Business Development Professional
- Trust Property Manager
- Trust Risk Analyst
- Workers' Compensation Analyst

Healthcare

Healthcare JD Advantage jobs are among the most dynamic and wide-ranging law-related careers. They are constantly evolving, usually by accretion—adding new issues to the mix that compel lawmakers to scramble in order to keep pace. The field is incredibly diverse, replete with numerous subspecialties.

Nontraditional healthcare legal arenas are expanding rapidly. Hospitals and other healthcare providers confront the same array of problems that other corporations face, such as corporate governance, employee relations and transactional matters, plus additional issues unique to their industry.

Both the federal and state governments are struggling to implement provisions of the Affordable Care Act and regulate emerging healthcare technologies while controlling costs. *Caveat: At this writing, the Affordable Care Act is in danger of massive revision or repeal.*

In addition to profitability, five metrics underscore healthcare JD Advantage opportunities:

- Healthcare reform.
- The dramatic growth of health law professional organizations, such as the American Health Lawyers Association; American College of Legal Medicine; American Society of Law, Medicine and Ethics; American Society for Healthcare Risk Management; and the Health Care Compliance Association, all of which have increased their membership rolls substantially in recent years, a sure sign of a strong and expanding field.
- The large number of health law seminars, Continuing Legal Education programs, conferences and such, and the premium price charged for many of these programs.

- A great deal of positioning and repositioning going on within the health law community, which will continue for many years.
- New technologies, such as telemedicine and e-prescribing, plus treatment breakthroughs, new drugs, etc., that arrive fraught with cutting-edge legal, regulatory, ethical, business, and other issues yet to be resolved.

The potential employer pool is enormous and includes academic medical centers, ambulatory care facilities, assisted living facilities, clinical laboratories, continuing care retirement communities, diagnostic facilities, dialysis companies, insurers, e-health companies, HMOs, health plans, healthcare systems, home healthcare agencies, hospices, hospitals, imaging services providers, long-term care facilities, medical equipment companies, nursing homes, PPOs, physician-based entities, physician practice management companies, physician practices, pharmaceutical firms, pharmacists, benefits managers, and trade and professional associations.

Selected JD Advantage Job Titles

- Bioethicist
- Contract Negotiator
- Director, Pharmaceutical Sales & Marketing Compliance
- Ethics Specialist
- Health Plan Member Services Coordinator
- Healthcare Compliance Officer
- Health Care Ombudsman

- HIPAA/Privacy Officer
- Hospital Planned Giving Professional
- Hospital Contracts/Procurement Officer
- Hospital Risk Manager
- JCAHO Policy Writer
- Legal Nurse Consultant
- Legal Services Specialist
- Patient Rights Advocate
- Workers' Compensation Claims   Adjudicator

Positioning Yourself for a Corporate JD Advantage Job

The tremendous and growing diversity of JD Advantage jobs in corporations means that your undergraduate, law school, and perhaps graduate educational background offers you many opportunities to hone your knowledge and skills for a particular type of position or corporate function. Hopefully, this booklet can provide you with guidance as to which areas might be both most promising and of greatest interest to you.

In addition, it is never a bad idea to add some heft to your resume and *bona fides* through (1) supplementing your education with either an additional degree or one or more far less expensive and less time-consuming certificate, professional development, or comparable programs, and (2) joining one or more relevant membership organizations in the field in which you are interested. A discussion of both "add-ons" follows.

Supplementing Your Education

Back in my company days, one of my clients, a recent law school grad, took my advice to supplement her JD with an online course geared toward an Associate in Risk Management (ARM) certificate offered by the American Insurance Institute (today known as The Institutes). It was a three-level course with an examination at the conclusion of each level. Once she passed the third level, she was awarded the ARM designation. The course cost just under $1,000, consisted of self-study materials, and took her three months of evenings to complete. She added the designation to her resume, grabbing immediate employer attention by first citing it at the very top of her document, i.e., "**JANE DOE, JD, ARM**" and began submitting applications for risk management positions in universities, hospitals, and municipal governments. Prior to garnering the ARM, she had spent many months following law school graduation mired in a frustrating and fruitless search for mainstream attorney jobs. The ARM changed that. She suddenly found herself in high demand and was invited to a series of interviews. She ended up accepting a job offer with a 300-bed hospital in a small Northeastern city.

Before you sign up for any program, you have to do two things:

First, determine the "opportunity cost." Will you be better off, job and career-wise, pursuing supplemental education, than you would be launching yourself immediately into the workforce, assuming you can secure the kind of job you are seeking or a transitional position that can eventually lead to where you want to go?

This is not that tough a comparative analysis if the alternative to working right now is a certificate or comparable program since these, like Jane Doe's, don't take much time, are reasonably priced, and can often be done while working or full-time job-hunting. With respect to these programs, the real question is their job and career-enhancement (read: resume-building) value. This is where your second task (see below) comes into play.

The closer question is whether investing the typically large tuition fees for a full-blown graduate degree are worth the cost and lost opportunity. Answering this question will require your best due diligence efforts.

Second, get a second, third, and fourth opinion of the program's true value. In either case, talk to the following individuals and ask them their opinion of the program's value and, in the case of program providers, what they will do to assist your career aspirations during and after you complete their program:

- Individuals who have earned the credential.
- Employers of individuals who recently earned the credential.
- Current students.
- Career placement professionals and program directors at the sponsoring school or organization.
- Outside organizations that monitor, report on, or rank programs you are considering.

Selected List of Supplemental "JD Advantage" Programs

Note: Certain programs require that enrollees have a requisite amount of experience in the field. Some others require membership in the provider organization as a prerequisite to enrollment.

In-House Counsel

Association of Legal Administrators (https://alanet.org/clm) Certified Legal Manager

Knowledge Management Institute (http://kminstitute.org)
    Certified Knowledge Practitioner/Specialist/Manager
    (three separate designations)
    Certified Knowledge Manager (onsite or online)

Corporate Governance

Sarbanes-Oxley Association (http://sarbanes-oxley-association.com)
    Certified Sarbanes Oxley Expert (online)
Harvard Business School Executive Education
(https://www.exed.hbs.edu)
    Corporate Governance Series
Northwestern University Kellogg School of Business
(http://kellogg.northwestern.edu/executive-education)
    Corporate Governance: Effectiveness and
    Accountability in the Boardroom

Tax

Georgetown Law School (https://www.law.georgetown.edu)
    Certificate Program in International Taxation (online or
    onsite)
New York University School of Law (http://law.nyu.edu)
    Advanced Professional Certificate in Taxation
Bentley College (http://bentley.edu)
    Advanced Professional Certificate in Taxation
Golden Gate University (http://ggu.edu/programs/
taxation/graduate-certificate-in-taxation)
    Graduate Certificate in Taxation (online or onsite)

Compliance

University of Toledo Law School (http://utoledo.edu/law)
    Graduate Certificate in Compliance (hybrid onsite/online)
International Association of Risk and Compliance Professionals (http://risk-compliance-association.com)
    Certified Risk and Compliance Management Professional (CRCMP) (online)
Society of Corporate Compliance & Ethics (http://corporatecompliance.org)
    Certified Compliance and Ethics Professional (self-study followed by an online test option)
    Certified Compliance and Ethics Professional-International (self-study followed by an online test option)
    Certified in Healthcare Compliance (self-study followed by an online test option)
    Certified in Healthcare Privacy Compliance (self-study followed by an online test option)
Financial Institutions Regulatory Agency
    Compliance Boot Camp (http://finra.org)
Lorman (http://lorman.com) – more than 25 diverse compliance programs available in multiple formats.
International Import-Export Institute (http://expandglobal.com) (online)
    Certified U.S. Import Compliance Officer®
    Certified U.S. Export Compliance Officer®

Risk Management

The prestigious online Associate in Risk Management certificate and examination program is offered by a number of organizations that have been licensed by The Institutes, including:

AB Training Center (http://abtrainingcenter.com)
    Associate in Risk Management (online)
KEIR Educational Resources (http://keirsuccess.com)
    Associate in Risk Management (online)
Insurance Educational Association (http://ieatraining.com)
    Associate in Risk Management (online)

The following selected risk management certificate and comparable programs are also available:

Boston University (http://bu.edu/online/programs/
certificate-programs/risk-management-organizational-
continuity)
    Online Graduate Certificate in Risk Management and
Organizational Continuity
Compliance LLC (http://compliance-llc.com)
    Certified Risk and Compliance Management
    Professional (online)
    Certified Risk and Compliance Management
    Professional in Insurance and Reinsurance   (online)
Global Association of Risk Professionals (http://garp.com)
    Financial Risk Manager (FRM) Certification
    Energy Risk Professional (ERM) Certification

American Hospital Association Certification Center
(http://aha.org)
　　Certified Professional in Healthcare Risk Management
　　(online)
International Risk Management Institute (http://irmi.com)
　　Construction Risk and Insurance Specialist (online)
University of Maryland (http://umd.edu)
　　Graduate Certificate of Professional Studies in Food
　　Safety Risk Analysis (online)
California State University, Bakersfield (http://csub.edu)
　　Occupational Safety and Risk Management Certificate
Institute of Consumer Financial Information
(http://icfe.info)
　　Certified Identity Theft Risk Management Specialist
　　(online)

Ethics

University of New Mexico
(https://mgtcert.mgt.unm.edu/upcoming-programs/
business-ethics.asp)
　　Business Ethics Online
Society of Corporate Compliance & Ethics
(http://corporatecompliance.org)
　　Certified Compliance & Ethics Professional

Due Diligence

International Due Diligence Association
(http://diligenceassociation.org/certification)
　　Certified Due Diligence Practitioner Program (online)

Florida Atlantic University College of Business
(http://business.fau.edu)
   Certificate in Financial Due Diligence (online or onsite)

Technology Commercialization

Licensing Executives Society
(http://licensingcertification.org)
   LES Professional Development Series
   Certified Licensing Professional Program
University of California, Berkeley Extension
(http://extension.berkeley.edu)
   Certificate in Technology Transfer and
   Commercialization
Courses for New Licensing and Non-Licensing Professionals
   IP Business Basics 101
   IP & Licensing Basics: A One-Day Review

Real Estate

New York University (http://www.sps.nyu.edu/
academics/departments/schack/academic-offerings/
graduate/ms-in-real-estate.html
   Graduate Certificate in Real Estate (onsite or online)
Drexel University (http://drexel.com/online-degrees/
business-degrees/cert-realestate/index.aspx)
   Graduate Certificate in Real Estate (online)
UCLA Extension (http://uclaextension.edu)
   Certificate in Business Administration with
   Concentration in Real Estate (online)

Litigation Management

Claims and Litigation Management Alliance
(http://theclm.org)
Certified Litigation Management Professional

Marketing

Legal Marketing Association (http://legalmarketing.org/
lma-cic)
LMA Competitive Intelligence Certificate

Intellectual Property

See also Technology Commercialization, above.

University of New Hampshire Law Center (http://unh.edu)
Intellectual Property Program (blended program: onsite
and online)
World Intellectual Property Organization (http://wipo.int)
WIPO Academy Online Programs (multiple programs on
a variety of IP topics)

Government Affairs

Georgetown University Government Affairs Institute
(http://gai.georgetown.edu)
Certificate Program in Legislative Studies
Congressional Operations Seminar

Women in Government Relations (http://wgr.org)
 Step into Power: Practical Leadership Skills
 Leadership Institutes
State Government Affairs Council (http://sgac.org/
professional-certificate-program.html)
 Professional Certificate Program

Contracting and Procurement

National Contract Management Association
(http://ncmahq.org)
 Certified Commercial Contracts Manager
 Certified Federal Contracts Manager
University of Virginia (http://virginia.edu)
 Graduate Certificate in Procurement and Contracts
 Management (online)
U.S. Small Business Administration
(https://sba.gov/tools/sba-learning-center/search/training)
(a large number of online courses on contracting and
business)

Acquisitions

See also Due Diligence, above.

MIT Open Courseware (https://ocw.mit.edu/courses/
sloan-school-of-management)
 The Law of Mergers and Acquisitions (online)
SMU Cox School of Business (http://smu.edu/Cox/
ExecutiveEducation/ProfessionalDevelopment)
 Mergers and Acquisitions

Privacy/Data Protection

International Association of Privacy Professionals
(http://iapp.org)
- Certified Information Privacy Professional/U.S. Private Sector (CIPP/US)
- Certified Information Privacy Professional/Government (CIPP/G)
- Certified Information Privacy Professional/Government/Europe (CIPP/E)
- Certified Information Privacy Manager (CIPM)

Institute of Consumer Financial Information (http://icfe.us)
- Certified Identity Theft Risk Management Specialist

Syracuse University (http://cybersecuritylaw.us and http://insct.syr.edu/academicprograms/cybersecurityonlinecourse)
- Cyber Security Law & Policy (online)

SANS Institute (http://SANS.org)
- Law of Data Security and Investigations (onsite or online)

Labor Relations

Cornell University School of Industrial and Labor Relations (http://ilr.cornell.edu/human-capital-development/certificates/labor-relations)
- Collective Bargaining Studies Certificate
- [Labor] Contract Administration Studies Certificate

Rutgers University (http://rutgers.edu)
    Labor and Employment Relations Certificate
    Diversity and Inclusion in the Workplace Certificate

Policy Management

Northwestern School of Professional Studies
(http://sps.northwestern.edu/program-areas/
advanced-graduate/policy-analysis) (onsite or online)
    Advanced Certificate in Policy Analysis
University of North Dakota (http://und.edu/academics/
extended-learning/online-distance/graduate-
certificates/policy-analysis)
    Graduate Certificate in Policy Analysis (online)

Human Resources

Cornell University (http://ecornell.com)
    Human Resources Essentials Certificate (online)
    Human Resources Management Certificate (online)
    Social Media in HR: From Policy to Practice (online)
Southern New Hampshire University (http://snhu.edu)
    Human Resource Management Certificate (online)
Institute for Applied Management and Law (http://iaml.com)
    Certificate in Employee Relations Law Seminar
    Certificate in Essentials of Human Resource
    Management Seminar
    Certificate in Conducting Lawful Workplace
    Investigations Seminar
    Certificate in Employee Benefits Law Seminar

Diversity

University of Colorado-Colorado Springs (http://uccs.edu/lases/diversity.html)
Graduate Certificate Program in Diversity, Social Justice and Inclusion
Georgetown University (http://scs.georgetown.edu/programs/396/strategic-diversity-and-inclusion-management)
Strategic Diversity and Inclusion Management Certificate
Cornell University Industrial & Labor Relations School (https://ilr.cornell.edu/human-capital-development/certificates)

Training

Training from the Back of the Room (http://bowperson.com)
Various Training Programs and Self-Study Literature
Texas A&M University (http://tamu.edu)
Training & Development Professional Certification
American College of Education (http://explore.ace.edu)
Certificate in Adult Education and Corporate Training
Association for Talent Development (https://td.org/Education/Programs/Training-Certificate)
Training Certificate
American Management Association (http://amanet.org)
Train the Trainer Seminars (3 days, multiple locations)

Joining a Membership Organization

The value of membership in organizations of like-minded individuals is considerable for legal job-seekers. One of the principal reasons such organizations exist is to allow members to network with each other for job prospects and alerts as to employers who might be hiring. In addition, membership organizations offer job seekers the opportunity to connect with both prospective employers and potentially valuable intermediaries.

Note. Some of the organizations listed below have special qualification requirements, such as time in the profession, or a requirement that a new member be nominated or sponsored for membership by one or more current members.

Selected JD Advantage Membership Organizations

General

American Society for Pharmacy Law (http://aspl.org)
Association of Corporate Counsel (http://acc.com)
American Bar Association Business Law Section (http://americanbar.org/groups/business_law.html)
American College of Construction Lawyers (http://accl.org)
Commercial Law League of America (http://clla.org)
Energy Bar Association (http://eba-net.org)
American Health Lawyers Association (http://healthlawyers.org)
International Association of Entertainment Lawyers (http://iael.org)

Federation of Defense & Corporate Counsel
(http://thefederation.org)
Food and Drug Law Institute (http://fdli.org)
International Media Lawyers Association
(http://internationalmedialawyers.org)
National Association of Railroad Trial Counsel
(http://nartc.org)
Sports Lawyers Association (http://sportslaw.org)
Association of Transportation Law Professionals
(http://atlp.org)
Transportation Lawyers Association (http://translaw.org)

Board of Directors Staff

American Society of Corporate Secretaries (http://ascs.org)
Sarbanes Oxley Compliance Professionals Association
(http://sarbanes-oxley-association.com)
Society of Corporate Secretaries & Governance
Professionals (http://governanceprofessionals.org/home)

Tax

American Association of Attorney-Certified Public
Accountants (http://attorney-cpa.com)
American Bar Association Taxation Section
(http://americanbar.org/groups/taxation.html)
American College of Tax Counsel (http://actonline.org)
Institute for Professionals in Taxation (http://ipt.org)
International Tax Planning Association (http://itpa.org)
National Association of Enrolled Agents (http://naea.org)

National Association of Tax Practitioners
(http://natptax.com)

Compliance

American Bar Association Section of Administrative Law
and Regulatory Practice (http://americanbar.org/groups/
administrative_law.html)
Association of Insurance Compliance Professionals
(http://aicp.net)
Association of Trade Compliance Professionals
(http://complianceprofessionals.org)
Ethics and Compliance Officers Association
(https://berkleycenter.georgetown.edu/organizations/
ethics-compliance-officer-association)
Federation of Regulatory Counsel (http://forc.org)
International Association of Risk and Compliance
Professionals (http://risk-compliance-association.com)
Regulatory Compliance Association
(http://regulatorycomplianceassociation.com)
Sarbanes Oxley Compliance Professionals Association
(http://sarbanes-oxley-association.com)
Society of Corporate Compliance & Ethics
(http://corporatecompliance.org)

Risk Management

American Society for Healthcare Risk Management
(http://ashrm.org)
Association of Insurance & Risk Managers
(http://airmic.com)

International Association of Risk & Compliance Professionals (http://risk-compliance-association.com)
Professional Risk Managers International Association (http://prmia.org)
Risk and Insurance Management Society, Inc. (http://rims.org)

Ethics

Ethics and Compliance Officers Association (https://berkleycenter.georgetown.edu/organizations/ethics-compliance-officer-association)

Due Diligence

Association of Due Diligence Professionals (http://manta.com/c/mxcyddb/association-of-due-diligence-professionals)
Association of Strategic Alliance Professionals (http://strategic-alliances.org)
International Due Diligence Association (http://diligenceassociation.org)

Technology Commercialization

Alliance of Technology Transfer Professionals (http://attp.info)
International Technology Law Association (http://itechlaw.org)
Licensing Executives Society (http://lesusacanada.org)

Real Estate

Association of Eminent Domain Professionals (http://www.aedp.org)
American Bar Association Real Property, Trust and Estate Law Section (http://americanbar.org/groups/real_property_trust_estate.html)
American College of Real Estate Lawyers (http://acrel.org)
Commercial Real Estate Development Association (http://naiop.org)
Counselors of Real Estate (http://cre.org)
International Association of Corporate Real Estate Executives (http://nacore.org)
Pension Real Estate Association (http://prea.org)

Litigation Management

Claims and Litigation Management Alliance (http://theclm.org)
National Association of Legal Fee Analysis (http://thenalfa.org)
Enterprise Content Management Association (http://aiim.org)

Marketing

Customs and International Trade Bar Association (http://citba.org)
Legal Marketing Association (http://legalmarketing.org)

Intellectual Property

Alliance of Technology Transfer Professionals
(http://attp.info)
American Bar Association Intellectual Property Law Section
(http://americanbar.org/groups/
intellectual_property_law.html)
American Intellectual Property Law Association
(http://aipla.org)
Copyright Society of America (http://csusa.org)
International Federation of Intellectual Property Attorneys
(http://ficpi.org)
International Institute for IP Management (http://i3pm.org)
International Trademark Association (http://inta.org)
Licensing Executives Society (http://lesusacanada.org)
National Association of Patent Practitioners
(http://napp.org)

Government Affairs

Public Affairs Council (http://pac.org)
Women in Government Relations (http://wgr.org)
State Government Affairs Council (http://sgac.org)

Contracting and Procurement

American Bar Association Public Contract Law Section
(http://americanbar.org/groups/public_contract_law.html)
Board of Contract Appeals Bar Association
(http://bcaba.org)

National Contract Management Association (http://ncmahq.org)

Acquisitions

Alliance of Merger & Acquisition Advisors (http://amaaonline.com)
Association of Professional Mergers and Acquisitions Advisors (http://apmaa.com)
Institute for Mergers, Acquisitions, and Alliances (https://imaa-institute.org)

Privacy/Data Protection

Cyberlaw Association (http://cyberlawassociation.com)
Cyberspace Bar Association (http://cyberbar.net)
International Association of Privacy Professionals (https://iapp.org)

Labor Relations

American Bar Association Labor and Employment Law Section (http://americanbar.org/groups/labor_law.html)
Labor and Employment Relations Association (http://leraweb.org)

Policy Management

American Constitution Society for Law and Policy (http://acslaw.org)

Association for Public Policy Analysis & Management (http://appam.org)

Human Resources

National Employment Lawyers Association (http://nela.org)
Society for Human Resource Management (http://shrm.org)

Diversity

American Association for Access, Equity and Diversity (https://aaaed.org/aaaed/Diversity_Management2.asp)
National Diversity Council (http://nationaldiversitycouncil.org)

What Do Corporate JD Advantage Jobs Pay?

The answers to this question are short and simple: It depends...on the size of the company, the nature of the position, the geographic location where you are working, and the demand for your particular knowledge, background, and skill set.

Certain types of JD Advantage jobs in companies are highly likely to pay more than others. For example, if you work in a position in Data Protection, which has companies panicking, you will probably be offered a handsome salary. Similarly, fields like Risk Management, Compliance, Corporate Governance, Due Diligence, Acquisitions, and Tax, to name a few, pay pretty well. In contrast, you may earn less initially if you work in Diversity Human Resources, or Contracting and Procurement.

One of the better ways of determining very general salary ranges is to contact one or more of the trade or professional associations representing companies and individuals in the fields in which you are interested and pose the salary question to them. They are likely to have the most up-to-date, accurate information about such matters.

Advance Notice of Corporate JD Advantage Opportunities

The legal job seeker's ultimate "inside information" is to be able to identify job opportunities in advance of any public notice of a job ad. Knowing who will be hiring and for what jobs before everyone else gives you an invaluable leg up on the competition. It enables you to be "first past the post" by getting your application into the employer before the competition and before a job ad or vacancy announcement hits the Internet. There are a number of ways to get this information.

The first several suggestions that follow focus on the gold mine that is the U.S. government when it comes to sources of this kind of information. What you need to do when you come across this information is *extrapolate what you learn from its public sector orientation to what it means for private sector (read: corporate) job and career opportunities.*

Congressional appropriations subcommittee testimony. Every spring, senior U.S. government department and agency officials appear before Senate and House appropriations subcommittees to explain, usually in considerable detail, their budget requests for the next fiscal year. Often, they "drill down" into the particulars, sometimes even to where they specify the number of new legal and law-related positions they seek and also elaborate on what their new hires will be doing. This is where what I call *Hermann's Corollary to Newton's Third Law of Motion* comes into play: You might recall from high school Physics that Sir Isaac's Third Law reads like this: *For every action,* *there is an equal and opposite reaction.* My Corollary refines the Third Law to read like this: *For every government action, there is a private sector reaction that is orders of magnitude greater than the original action.*

When you apply the Corollary, forget about the number of public sector jobs the government's initiative or policy announcement might be generating. What is important for you is its impact on attorney and JD Advantage job creation in companies affected by the action. Here's an example from a recent year's testimony by the Chair of the Commodity Futures Trading Commission (CFTC) (http://cftc.gov) before the Senate Appropriations Committee's Subcommittee on Financial Services and General Government:

- *Strengthening the Commission's Enforcement Program.* The CFTC should be adequately resourced to vigorously investigate and litigate complex market manipulation and trade-practice violations. *Adequate legal staff is necessary to act swiftly to investigate and prosecute fraudulent acts,* such as the rash of Ponzi schemes uncovered during the market downturn.

- *Rigorously Exercising Existing Authorities to Ensure Market Integrity. Additional economic and legal staff* will enable the CFTC to conduct mandatory annual reviews of all contracts listed on exempt commercial markets to determine if they are significant price discovery contracts. Specifically, the funding will be allocated to increase staffing levels in the following divisions:

- **Enforcement.** The Commission's Enforcement program is on track to reach a staff level of more than 170 by the end of this fiscal year. This is a significant program turnaround from an all-time low of 109 in FY 2008. Nevertheless, a staff of 170 may be below what is needed to address the current challenges brought by the recent financial crisis. Our goal is to have an Enforcement staff of 200, including strategic plans to double the Enforcement staff in the Kansas City office.

- **Market Oversight.** The rapid changes occurring in the futures markets over the last decade have brought new challenges to [this Division]. DMO now needs additional experienced professional staff to actively monitor exchanges to ensure compliance with CFTC regulations and seeks to increase [the Division's] staff from 139 to 168, specifically economists, investigators, attorneys and statisticians.

- **Clearing and Intermediary Oversight.** Additional resources would allow the Commission to perform regular and direct examinations of registrants and more frequently assess compliance with Commission regulations. The Commission seeks to increase the Division of Clearing and Intermediary Oversight staff from 113 to 120.

- **Offices of the Chairman and the Commissioners.** The Offices of the Chairman and the Commissioners require professional, legal and economic expertise as they undertake a number of high priority programmatic initiatives, including: 1) subject to enactment of new authorities, regulation of derivatives markets and regulatory changes to protect the American public from systemic financial risks; 2) regulatory coordination with other agencies such as the Securities and Exchange Commission (SEC) and Federal Energy Regulatory Commission (FERC); 3) promoting market transparency; 4) promoting transparency on the Commission's website; 5) regulation of energy markets; 6) increasing frequency of reviews and audits of Commission registrants; and 7) technology modernization, resource justification and program performance. The Commission proposes to bolster these offices from 35 to 47 staff.

- Enterprise Risk Management Office. The budget proposes a new Enterprise Risk Management subprogram, consisting of three staff, to focus on proactively developing and employing methods and processes to manage risks that may be obstacles to the discharge of the Commission's responsibilities.
- Office of International Affairs. The budget requests an additional staff member in the Office of International Affairs, which coordinates the Commission's non-enforcement related international activities, represents the Commission in international organizations, coordinates Commission policy as it relates to U.S.

Treasury global initiatives, and provides technical assistance to foreign market authorities.

- *Regulatory Reform.* The Commission's budget request includes *an additional $45,000,000 and 119 full-time equivalent employees to [continue] implementation of the [Dodd-Frank Act].* Specifically, the budget request for regulatory reform would be allocated as follows:
  - 41 additional staff for Market Oversight;
  - 30 additional staff for Clearing and Intermediary Oversight and Risk Surveillance;
  - 18 additional staff for Enforcement;
  - 15 additional staff for Information Technology;
  - Eight additional staff for General Counsel;
  - Five additional staff for Human Resources and Management Operations;
  - One additional staff for the Chief Economist;
  - And one additional staff for International Affairs.

As you can see, this is an information bonanza about what the CFTC planned to do in the coming fiscal year. Just to take one facet of the testimony, stepped up enforcement meant that regulated entities were compelled to bolster their legal and compliance staffs. They did that in a very big way.

The CFTC regulates several thousand commodity contract markets, swap execution facilities, derivatives clearing organizations, swap data repositories, swap dealers, futures commission merchants, commodity pool operators and other intermediaries. These include markets and contracts on energy and metals commodities, such as crude oil, heating oil, gasoline, copper, gold and silver; contracts on financial products, such as interest rates, stock indexes and foreign currency; and since the 2008 financial crisis, the swaps market, which is about 12 times the size of the futures market.

Every single one of these regulated entities is subject to the policy pronouncements and regulatory initiatives that the CFTC Chair cited in his appropriations subcommittee testimony, above. That translated to an enormous number of legal job opportunities in regulated entities, *few if any of which would have been public knowledge at the time of the testimony.*

Testimony transcripts are typically available on committee websites.

The most important point about this "early warning system" is this: When you read this testimony, note that even if it does not drill all the way down to specific position numbers, you are likely to find evidence of policy and regulatory initiatives and shifts that will alert you that new or additional corporate hires might be required in order to implement new compliance and risk management projects and programs. This is where your analytical and "dot-connection" skills come into play. *Every government initiative invariably leads to private sector responses that generate multiples—often by orders of magnitude—of any new federal jobs. This is especially true of regulatory agencies.*

For corporate JD Advantage jobs, you will want to monitor those federal departments and agencies that regulate or otherwise impact on the fields in which you are interested. I won't list them here because virtually every U.S. government organization has some role with respect to private sector companies.

You can also apply *Hermann's Corollary* to the following government early information alerts:

Government Annual Performance Plans and Strategic Plans. These can also be mined for "hidden" corporate legal job opportunities. Annual Performance Plans and Strategic Plans are, prepared and published on department and agency websites each year and every 3-5 years, respectively. These legally-required documents are more "hit-or-miss" when it comes to ferreting out specific corporate legal job opportunities than appropriations subcommittee testimony. However, you can almost always get a sense of the direction in which the agency is moving and the issues they deem top priority.

Proposed federal and state legislation. It won't take you long to review bills that have been introduced in Congress and state legislatures that have serious legal job generation potential, given Congress's light workload (In 2016 your representatives bothered to meet only 111 days...nice "work" if you can get it) and inability to get much done. Go to http://congress.gov and search for relevant key words. Don't waste much time on bills where it is clear that they are going nowhere. You can do similar searches at comparable state legislative websites.

For example, the *Affordable Care Act* and *Dodd-Frank Act* created several thousand new U.S. government attorney and JD Advantage jobs, but at least several hundred times that number of new private sector jobs in the affected regulated entities.

State referenda and initiatives. Ballot initiatives and referenda are very interesting early indicators of legal job creation. Consider, for example, the six states that have now approved recreational marijuana, which is in the process of creating an entire new industry, including both a ton of new legal business and new corporate legal job opportunities.

Agency Semi-Annual Regulatory Agendas. Every spring and fall, U.S. government agencies publish their regulatory action priority lists in the *Federal Register* (http://federalregister.gov). These lists and accompanying explanations tell you what agencies think is important as well as which regulatory projects are likely to be proposed, undertaken, and/or finalized during the next six months. They also enable you to anticipate what might be coming with respect to corporate law hiring needs.

To cite one example, the Commerce Department announced in its November 2016 semi-annual regulatory agenda that, in mid-2017, it was going to propose an overhaul of certain technology licensing procedures with respect to federally-funded research under the *Bayh-Dole Act*. This is of critical importance to corporate (and other, e.g., university) technology commercialization offices. Savvy legal job seekers interested in this field could identify affected companies and factor this proposed rule into their marketing pitches.

Agency regulatory agendas are aggregated at the Reginfo.gov website (http://reginfo.gov), where you can examine pending regulatory projects agency-by-agency.

Federal budget documents. Examine the annual proposed *Budget of the United States*, best viewed at http://omb.gov. Forget about the actual budget itself, largely a collection of dizzying numerical data that excite only accountants and economists, but put everyone else into a stupor. Instead, examine each relevant department and agency's *Budget Appendix*. These are primarily textual documents that explain agency funding requests.

Governments are not the only sources of advance notice of potential corporate JD Advantage jobs. The following private-sector notice strategies are also at your disposal:

Take stock. Publicly-traded companies whose shares are steadily increasing in value (for non-speculative reasons) have a consistent history of hiring new employees for attorney and law-related jobs.

Hunt for profits. Scan newspaper and online tables showing quarterly earnings reports for companies that have increased their profits by more than five percent from the preceding year. This growth rate often presages a need for additional employees.

Study financials. Become a consistent and careful reader of financial publications. Mainstream media and investment newsletters contain a great deal of this kind of advance information about where jobs are likely to be in the near term. Certain publications, websites, and trade associations produce detailed annual reports that aggregate and present information about their industries. For example, A.M. Best (http://ambest.com) produces such reports about the financial health of insurance companies. Online, these reports are an expensive subscription product. You may be able to view them through your local central library either online or in print.

Identify new financings. Newspaper business/financial sections (e.g., *The Wall Street Journal* ([http://wsj.com], *Financial Times* [http://ft.com], *Bloomberg Business Week* [http://bloomberg.com/businessweek]), financial websites (e.g., *CNN Money* [http://money.cnn.com], *Hoovers* [http://hoovers.com], *Business Finance* [http://businessfinancemag.com], *Institutional* Investor [http://institutionalinvestor.com]), and industry trade journals (e.g., *Insurance Journal* [http://insurancejournal.com], *Best's Review* [http://bestreview.com]), often carry announcements of significant business financings. New financings often predate major expansions and a corresponding need for additional employees.

Join corporate and/or industry membership organizations. Like-minded companies and professionals invariably band together to enhance their professional development and business and job opportunities. One of the most important things you can learn about at organization meetings is pending job opportunities. One of the best such "umbrella" organizations is the Association of Corporate Counsel (http://acc.com).

All of these strategies make you a *proactive* rather than merely a *reactive* job-seeker. Moreover, by describing for a prospective employer (in your cover letter or transmittal email) just exactly how you anticipated its hiring needs gains you significant additional points for your creative intelligence, innovative approach, diligence, and foresight. Employers take serious notice of initiative that goes beyond the conventional approach to job-hunting.

A Word About Nonprofit Corporations

Note. Attorney and JD Advantage job opportunities in nonprofit corporations are addressed in Volume 13 of our 21st Century Legal Career Series. What follows is a brief "tickler."

The National Center for Charitable Statistics (http://nccs.urban.org) says that there are more than 1.6 million nonprofit organizations registered in the U.S. While nonprofits are not as fully vested in the JD Advantage "movement" as their commercial counterparts, there is nevertheless a lot of opportunity in this sector. The following types of nonprofits are the most active with respect to offering the largest number of JD Advantage jobs:

Trade and Professional Associations

The association legal market, after the government, was the largest employer of lawyers in the Washington, DC metropolitan area. Very few lawyers and law students are aware that trade and professional associations employ thousands of attorneys and individuals with legal training in a diverse and growing array of professional positions.

The IRS says that there are more than 90,000 U.S. trade and professional associations. Associations have insinuated themselves into all aspects of our lives. Associations are everywhere and do everything. There are few, if any, areas of American life that have not spawned at least one trade or professional association. Associations are formed to promote and advance the wellbeing of their members.

There are basically two kinds of associations:

Trade Associations. Organizations of business competitors who join together to boost their industry. Examples include: American Trucking Association, American Gas Association, American Hospital Association, American Bankers Association, and National Association of Home Builders.

Professional Associations. Professional societies of individuals with common subject-matter knowledge, e.g., medicine, economics, law. They exist for reasons similar to the rationale for trade associations. In addition to monitoring of, and representation before, government legislative and executive branches, they seek to advance the professionalism of their occupation and the career interests of individuals engaged in that profession.

Examples of well-known professional associations include: American Bar Association, American Medical Association, American Dental Association, American Arbitration Association, and Financial Planning Association.

The standing joke in Washington, DC is that, when two people or businesses—e.g., pet sitters who specialize in gerbils; bunny show judges—discover that they have shared interests, *voilà*, they form an association. In truth, it usually takes more than two to tango, associationally-speaking. But not many more.

The primary impetus for forming an association is to get a legislature or public agency to do something on the members' behalf—pass favorable legislation or issue a regulation that benefits your business or occupation; or, conversely, to repeal a law or withdraw a regulation that is unfavorable to members. Secondarily, to monitor what legislators and regulators are up to, and report to the membership thereon. Thirdly, to provide opportunities to exchange information and assist with marketing, promotion and branding of whatever it is the association is trying to "sell."

Geography

Associations can be found all over the U.S. However, there are high concentrations of them in the Washington, DC metropolitan area (approximately 13,000), Chicago (2,000+), New York, Houston and Los Angeles. Many of these happen to be national associations. National associations in large cities outside of Washington, DC often also maintain a Washington office. National and international associations may have state and local chapters. Regional, statewide, and even local associations can be found throughout the country.

While associations were, for years, a peculiarly American phenomenon, that is no longer the case. Today, you can find international associations all over the world, usually headquartered in major country national capitals. As globalization proceeds, expect more of this.

What Associations Do

Associations do virtually anything you can imagine. That may include fulfilling societal needs that government would otherwise have to meet.

Elaborating on both this statement and what was generally described above, associations typically engage in all or many of the following activities:

- They represent the interests of their members (lobby), before legislatures, government agencies, and the public.
- They promote member professionalism.
- They sponsor events, seminars, webinars and symposia for members.

Why Do Associations Hire Attorneys?

The principal reason why attorneys are prized is because so much of what associations do is infused by law. Lawyers are in the best position to serve in an array of association positions (see below) because they can perform so many of the missions that give rise to associations and keep them in business.

Where Lawyers Work in Associations

I've identified 15 different association roles (including the general counsel office) occupied by attorneys. This is, of course, not true of every association. The larger the association, the more likely you are to find attorneys in all or many of these diverse units.

116

Note. Subdivision and job title terminology can vary widely from one association to another.

- In-House Counsel Office
- Government Affairs/Relations
- Education and Training
- Ethics and Standards of Conduct
- Public Affairs
- Corporate Governance
- Compliance
- Campaign Finance/Political Action Committee
- State Licensing Matters
- Taxation
- Inter-Organizational Liaison Offices
- Policy Development & Analysis
- Specialized Law or Law-Related Divisions
- The Top Job
- Association Management Companies

Selected Association JD Advantage Job Titles

- Advocacy and Mobilization Director
- Area Manager-External Affairs
- Collective Impact and Policy Strategist
- Community Grassroots Specialist
- Community Liaison
- Congressional Affairs Officer
- Director of Government Affairs
- Emerging Issues Leader
- External Relations Manager

117

- Federal Liaison
- Global Government Affairs Director
- Government Affairs Officer
- Government Information Specialist
- Government Regulations and Relations Officer
- Government Relations Manager
- Government Relations Specialist
- Intergovernmental Relations Specialist
- Legislative Policy Professional
- Lobbyist
- Public Affairs Associate
- Public Policy Analyst
- State/Local Government Affairs Representative
- Strategic Communications Advisor
- Vice President of Public Affairs

Hospitals

There are 2,870 nonprofit hospitals, which accounts for just over half of the total number of U.S. hospitals. Both attorney and JD Advantage job opportunities in hospitals are growing rapidly. These institutions confront the same array of problems that other corporations face, only they are often more acute and time-sensitive, with much shorter windows for favorable resolution.

The Affordable Care Act (ACA) has changed the health law equation dramatically. As governments at the federal and state levels attempt to respond to growing public pressure to do something about a U.S. healthcare system that is generally deemed much too expensive (health care expenditures are rising at three times the rate of [pre-recession] inflation), broken (my own family physician will tell you this), and in need of massive overhaul (the World Health Organization ranks the U.S. healthcare system 37th, below such national healthcare luminaries as Colombia and Morocco), the number of both mainstream attorney and law-related positions is growing.

Five metrics underscore hospitals as a major expansion arena for JD Advantage jobs:

1. **The dramatic growth of healthcare law professional organizations**, all of which have increased their membership rolls substantially in recent years, a sure sign of a strong and expanding practice area.
2. **The large number of healthcare law seminars, Continuing Legal Education programs, conferences, etc.**, encompassing every conceivable healthcare law topic, and the premium price charged for many of these programs.
3. **Healthcare reform.** There is a great deal of positioning and repositioning going on within the healthcare legal community in an attempt to anticipate and take advantage of the opportunities and challenges resulting from the ACA and what might ensue under the Trump administration.
4. **New technologies**, such as telemedicine, e-prescribing, treatment breakthroughs, new drugs, etc., that arrive fraught with cutting-edge legal, regulatory, ethical, business and other issues yet to be resolved.

5. **Globalization**, which in a healthcare context, is a very bad development, consisting of the rapid planetary spread of drug-resistant and dangerous infectious diseases (Ebola, Zika, SARS, MERS, Avian Flu, etc.) combined with the diminishing effect of antibiotics.

Not every hospital or healthcare provider has an in-house legal staff. As a rough rule of thumb, hospitals with 200 or more beds are the most likely to have their own in-house legal offices. Hospitals of this size may also have a Risk Management Office, Compliance Department, Contract and Procurement Office, Ethics Office, Ombudsman Office and/or a Patient Rights and Advocacy Office. Note: As indicated above, the 200-bed rule of thumb is changing, as the implementation of the ACA (and what might evolve from it) moves forward and prompts smaller hospitals to seek additional legal expertise.

There are a large and growing number of healthcare law, policy, and advocacy organizations, research entities, "think tanks," foundations, universities, etc., that employ individuals with a legal background. Some of the more recent additions to this employment sector have been launched due to the growing clamor for healthcare reform from politicians, policy researchers and the consuming public.

Hospital JD Advantage Offices and Jobs

- Regulatory Compliance
- Risk Management
- Ethics/Bioethics
- Health Policy
- Government/Legislative Affairs

- Legal Nurse Consulting
- Research Integrity
- Health Technology Transfer
- Patient Rights Advocacy
- Claims
- Health Law Research And Writing
- Healthcare Privacy
- Healthcare Ombudsman

Other Healthcare Nonprofits

Policy and Research Organizations. The rise in significance of healthcare as a major policy issue and one crying out for overhaul has seen a corresponding rise in the number of healthcare policy and research organizations and "think tanks" eager to make their mark and get their points across in the ongoing debate.

Healthcare Trade and Professional Associations. Numerous healthcare trade and professional associations have a powerful presence in Washington, DC, in major state capitals (e.g., Boston, Hartford, Albany, Trenton, Harrisburg, Richmond, Raleigh, Atlanta, Tallahassee, Columbus, Springfield (IL), Lansing, St. Paul, Austin, Denver, Sacramento, Phoenix), and in the larger cities (e.g., New York, Philadelphia, Baltimore, Chicago, Cleveland, Kansas City, Los Angeles, San Francisco, Seattle). Many of them have a General Counsel office; all of them have Government Affairs/Relations offices; and some of them have Ethics offices that specialize in advising association members with respect to ethics and professional responsibility questions.

Advocacy Organizations. Most healthcare advocacy organizations have been around for some time and are organized around specific healthcare issues, regarding which they lobby legislators and regulators, file lawsuits and represent individuals, interest groups and or businesses in healthcare disputes.

Foundations. Healthcare-oriented foundations fund legal, policy and other projects designed to improve the health delivery system, and often have legal/healthcare-related staff to identify and administer projects.

Miscellaneous Healthcare Nonprofits. A variety of nonprofits do not fit neatly into one of the categories listed above. Examples include:
- Center for Practical Bioethics (http://practicalbioethics.org)
- Joint Commission on the Accreditation of Healthcare Organizations (http://jcaho.org)
- Kaiser Permanente (http://kaiserpermanente.org)
- National Academy of Social Insurance (http://nasi.org)
- National Health Law Program (http://www.healthlaw.org) A
- National Institute for Health Care Management (http://nihcm.org)
- National Insurance Crime Bureau (http://nicb.org)
- Project Hope (http://projecthope.org)
- Public Responsibility in Medicine and Research (http://primr.org)

For more detailed information about health law careers, see Volume 3, *Health Law: Career Opportunities in a Fast-Changing Environment*, in the *21st Century Legal Careers Series*, available in print from http://nalp.org/bookstore or digitally at http://legalcareerview.com.

Colleges and Universities

JD Advantage job opportunities have proliferated on America's almost 5,000 campuses to an extent far beyond any other employment sector. They include:

Teaching

Teaching in Law Schools. In addition to tenure-track positions (usually Assistant Professors, Associate Professors and full Professors), law schools hire non-tenure track teachers under job titles such as Instructor and Lecturer, Academic Support Instructor, Clinical Program Director, Legal Research & Writing Program Instructor, Adjunct Professor and a variety of others.

Teaching Law in Undergraduate and Graduate Programs. This is where the significant growth in teaching opportunities for lawyers exists. Hundreds of undergraduate institutions now offer a Legal Studies or comparable major to their students. There is also a strong market for attorneys in other, more traditional undergraduate and graduate departments, such as business, accounting, criminal justice and law enforcement, real estate, insurance, and international affairs, among others.

Teaching in Paralegal Programs. The rapid expansion of paralegal certificate programs also means more teaching positions for lawyers. Attorneys from a practice background predominate among paralegal program faculties. The American Bar Association has approved 260 paralegal programs. There are also a substantial number of non-ABA approved paralegal programs, as well as a growing number of online programs.

Teaching Law Abroad. English is rapidly becoming the "international" language, and even more so the *lingua franca* of international business. This development has given rise to a proliferation of law and law-related course and degree offerings – in English – by foreign academic institutions. There has been a corresponding increase in demand for U.S.-educated individuals as teachers by these institutions. Most such opportunities are found in the English-speaking world of common law countries, including: Canada, the United Kingdom, Australia, and New Zealand, followed by countries where English is a primary second language (India, South Africa, other former and present Commonwealth nations), and also by countries that are – or aspire to be – international business centers (e.g., Belgium, the Netherlands).

Continuing Legal Education Providers. Numerous nonprofit organizations provide continuing legal education (CLE) courses, spurred largely by the online revolution, as well as by the accelerating pace of change in the law and legal topical areas. These range from law schools to state, local and specialty bar associations.

Other Selected Legal and Law-Related Teaching and Training Options. This category includes public interest and advocacy organizations, as well as Non-Governmental Organizations (NGOs) and Self-Regulatory Organizations (SROs).

For more detailed information about law teaching careers, see Volume 10, *Law Teaching and Training: Law School and Way Beyond*, in the *21st Century Legal Careers Series*, available in print from http://nalp.org/bookstore or digitally at http://legalcareerview.com.

Education Administration

The nation's accredited colleges and universities also provide a richly diverse and expanding non-teaching environment for lawyers, thanks to two parallel trends that have heavily influenced campus legal hiring and staff development over the last 20 years:

- The establishment of in-house counsel offices and the subsequent bringing on campus of much of the legal work that used to be farmed out to law firms. Today, there are only a handful of four-year and two-year colleges and universities that do not have in-house counsel offices.

- The subsequent realization that, due to the increasing complexity of campus life combined with the insinuation of legal considerations into so many aspects of human endeavor, many legal and law-related staff functions required more specialized attention than they could receive from the campus general counsel's office. This realization has resulted in the separating out of the campus general counsel's office of certain specialized legal/law-related activities, such as:

- Equal Employment Opportunity and Affirmative Action
- Risk Management
- Technology Transfer and Licensing
- Contract Management
- Ethics
- Campus "Judicial" Affairs
- Environmental Matters
- Legislative and Regulatory Affairs
- Compliance
- Government Affairs
- Sponsored Research and Industry Alliances
- International Student Affairs
- Disabled Student Affairs
- Real Estate
- and others

Increasingly, colleges are being compelled to "legalize" their decision-making. Traditionally, the courts deferred to faculty and academic administrators. However, that principle is eroding. Matters traditionally confined to the academy have now become subjects of public scrutiny. Academic institutions find themselves embroiled in a growing number of disputes. In addition, legal issues on campus have pervaded numerous campus activities and behavior. Moreover, Federal and state government legal oversight and legal processes now reach much more deeply into academic institutions than ever before. Colleges have had to inaugurate extensive compliance programs in response to a barrage of government statutory and regulatory initiatives covering areas such as healthcare, fundraising, student loans, foreign students, students with disabilities, and records management.

For more detailed information about education law careers, see Volume 9, *The Education Sector: Overwhelmed by Law*, in the *21st Century Legal Careers Series*, available in print from http://nalp.org/bookstore or digitally at http://legalcareerview.com.

Follow-Up

The differentiation of corporate legal and quasi-legal functions has accomplished two things that should be of great interest to every attorney and law student who aspires to work in a corporate setting:

1. The opening up of corporate legal employment to recent law grads; and
2. The expansion of legal opportunities far beyond the in-house counsel office.

Selected Further Information Resources

- Society of Corporate Compliance and Ethics (http://corporatecompliance.org)
- Society of Corporate Secretaries & Governance Professionals (http://governanceprofessionals.org)
- Federation of Regulatory Counsel (http://forc.org)
- American Society of Law, Medicine and Ethics (http://aslme.org)
- Ethics and Compliance Officer Association https://berkleycenter.georgetown.edu/ organizations/ethics-compliance-officer-association
- Ethics Resource Center (http://ethics.org)
- Association of Insurance & Risk Managers (http://airmic.com)
- Global Association of Risk Professionals (http://garp.com)

- Professional Risk Managers International Association (http://prmia.org)
- Risk and Insurance Management Society, Inc. (http://rims.org)
- Risk Management Association (http://rmahq.org)
- American Society for Healthcare Risk Management (http://ashrm.org)
- Licensing Executives Society (http://lesusacanada.org)
- American Intellectual Property Law Association (http://aipla.org)
- International Trademark Association (http://inta.org)
- International Anti-Counterfeiting Coalition (http://iacc.org)
- World Intellectual Property Organization (http://wipo.int)
- World Trade Organization (http://wto.org)
- American College of Real Estate Lawyers (http://acrel.org)
- Counselors of Real Estate (http://cre.org)
- National Association of Real Estate Investment Trusts (http://nareit.org)
- Pension Real Estate Association (http://prea.org)
- Federation of Defense and Corporate Counsel (http://thefederation.org)
- Defense Research Institute (http://dri.org)
- Legal Marketing Association (http://legalmarketing.org)
- Law Marketing Portal (http://lawmarketing.com)
- Government Affairs Yellow Book (http://leadershipdirectories.com)
- Lobbyist Databases (http://opensecrets.org/lobby)
- Top Lobbying Firms (http://publicintegrity.org)

- Foreign Representatives Yellow Book (http://leadershipdirectories.com)
- National Contract Management Association (http://ncmahq.org)
- Turnaround Management Association (http://turnaround.org)
- Institute for Professionals in Taxation (http://ipt.org)
- International Tax Planning Association (http://itpa.org)
- National Association of Tax Practitioners (http://natptax.com)
- National Tax Association (http://ntanet.org)
- American Bar Association Section of Taxation (http://abanet.org/tax)
- Tax Analysts (http://taxanalysts.org)
- *The Art of M&A Due Diligence* by Alexandra Reed Lajoux, Charles M. Elson (available from McGraw Hill, Amazon, and Barnes and Noble).
- *Venture Capital Due Diligence* by Justin J. Camp (available from Wiley, Amazon, and Barnes and Noble).

21st Century Legal Career fields by their nature are constantly changing and responding to a variety of pressures including the political environment, technological innovation, globalization, etc. Updates from the author on the material contained in this booklet are posted at http://legalcareerview.com. *Find the new information for this title under the 21st Century Careers menu on the home page. Check the Updates link on that page frequently.*

Made in the USA
Middletown, DE
28 April 2017